The Ultimate
BARBECUE
Cookbook

The Ultimate
BARBECUE
Cookbook

Over 200 sizzling dishes for outdoor eating

Contributing Editor: Christine France

HERMES HOUSE

INTRODUCTION

However simple, there's something about the charbroiled flavor of barbecued food that makes it taste extra special. Maybe it owes part of its appeal to the fresh air that sharpens the appetite and makes that tantalizing aroma so totally irresistible.

There's nothing new about cooking over charcoal; in fact, it's a method of cooking that has been used in most civilizations throughout history. The basic method has changed little over the centuries, but many modern grills are very sophisticated, making the job easier, cleaner and more controllable. Whether you're cooking over a simple pile of sticks or on a state-of-the art gas grill, outdoor cooking is fun, easy and inexpensive.

There are disputes over the origin of the word "barbecue," but one explanation is that it comes from *barbacoa*, a Spanish-American word used by the Arawak tribe of the Caribbean as the name for the wooden frame that held their food over an open fire as it cooked. The Arawaks were cannibals, so the food we cook today is rather different from their offerings!

Whatever your tastes, this collection of recipes offers new, unusual ideas for your barbecue as well as some traditional favorites. There's something for every occasion, from family meals to entertaining: spicy, fruity and exotic grills using fish, meat and poultry; easy sauces and marinades to turn basic ingredients into something new and special; and luscious, indulgent desserts. For vegetarians, there's a whole chapter of innovative ideas that everyone will enjoy.

Best of all, not only does a barbecue set the cook free from the kitchen but, for once, everyone else will actually want to help with the cooking.

APPETIZERS AND SNACKS

———◆———

As everyone knows, there is nothing like the aroma of charbroiling food

to whet the appetite. To keep your guests happy while they are waiting

for the main event, begin your barbecue feast with exciting appetizers

that are quick to cook and fun to eat. Here is a collection of

flavorsome and colorful dishes that are guaranteed to disappear

from the grill rack as soon as they're cool enough to snatch away.

There are lots of creative recipes for finger foods to be nibbled with

drinks – from crisp potato skins to spicy spare ribs – with plenty of

interesting dips and sauces to dunk them in, as well as delicious

suggestions for elegant appetizers for more formal meals.

ROASTED GARLIC TOASTS

Roasting garlic in its skin on a grill produces a soft, aromatic purée with a sweet, nutty flavor.
Spread on crisp toast to make a delicious appetizer or accompaniment to meat or vegetable dishes.

INGREDIENTS

2 whole garlic heads
extra virgin olive oil
fresh rosemary sprigs
loaf of ciabatta or thick baguette
chopped fresh rosemary
salt and freshly ground black
pepper

SERVES 4

1 Slice the tops from the heads of garlic using a sharp kitchen knife.

2 Brush the garlic heads with extra virgin olive oil and add a few sprigs of fresh rosemary before wrapping in foil. Cook the foil parcels on a medium-hot grill for 25–30 minutes, turning occasionally, until the garlic is soft.

3 Slice the bread and brush each slice generously with olive oil. Toast the slices on the grill until crisp and golden, turning once.

4 Squeeze the garlic cloves from their skins onto the toasts. Sprinkle with the chopped fresh rosemary and olive oil, and add salt and black pepper to taste.

ROASTED PEPPER ANTIPASTO

. . .

Jars of Italian mixed peppers in olive oil are a common sight in supermarkets, yet none can compete with this freshly made version, perfect as an appetizer or served with cold cuts.

INGREDIENTS

3 red bell peppers
2 yellow or orange bell peppers
2 green bell peppers
½ cup sun-dried tomatoes in oil, drained
1 garlic clove
2 tablespoons balsamic vinegar
5 tablespoons olive oil
few drops of chili sauce
4 canned artichoke hearts, drained and sliced
salt and freshly ground black pepper
fresh basil leaves, to garnish

SERVES 6

1 Cook the whole peppers on a medium-hot grill, turning frequently, for 10–15 minutes, until they begin to char. Cover the grilled peppers with a clean dish towel and allow them to cool for 5 minutes.

2 Use a sharp kitchen knife to slice the sun-dried tomatoes into thin strips. Thinly slice the garlic clove.

3 Whisk together the balsamic vinegar, olive oil and chili sauce in a small bowl, then season with a little salt and freshly ground black pepper.

4 Cut off the stalks and slice the peppers. Mix with the artichokes, sun-dried tomatoes and garlic. Add the dressing and sprinkle with basil leaves.

HERB-STUFFED MINI-VEGETABLES

These little hors d'oeuvres are ideal for parties, as they can be prepared in advance and simply assembled and cooked at the last minute.

INGREDIENTS

30 mini-vegetables: zucchini, pattypan squash and large button mushrooms
2 tablespoons olive oil
fresh basil or parsley, to garnish

FOR THE STUFFING
2 tablespoons olive oil
1 onion, finely chopped
1 garlic clove, finely chopped
4 ounces button mushrooms, finely chopped
1 zucchini, finely chopped
1 red bell pepper, finely chopped
1/3 cup orzo pasta or long-grain rice
1/3 cup tomato sauce
1/2 teaspoon dried thyme
1/2 cup chicken stock
1-2 teaspoons chopped fresh basil or parsley
2 ounces mozzarella or fontina cheese, coarsely grated
salt and freshly ground black pepper

MAKES 30

1 For the stuffing, heat the oil in a pan over medium heat. Add the onion and cook for 2 minutes, until tender. Stir in the garlic, mushrooms, zucchini and red pepper. Season and cook for 2 minutes, until the vegetables soften.

2 Stir in the pasta or rice, the tomato sauce, thyme and stock and bring to a boil, stirring. Reduce the heat and simmer for 10–12 minutes, until reduced and thickened. Remove from the heat and let cool slightly. Stir in the basil or parsley and the cheese.

3 Drop the zucchini and squash into boiling water and cook for 3 minutes. Drain and refresh under cold running water. Trim the bottoms so they are flat, trim a small slice off the tops and scoop out the centers with a spoon or melon baller. Remove the stems from the mushrooms. Brush all of the vegetables with olive oil.

4 Using a teaspoon, fill the vegetables with the stuffing and arrange on a rack. Cook on a medium-hot grill or broil for 10–15 minutes, until the filling is hot and bubbling. Garnish with fresh basil or parsley. The vegetables can be served either warm or at room temperature.

POLPETTE WITH MOZZARELLA AND TOMATO

. . .

*These Italian-style meatballs are made with beef and topped with creamy melted
mozzarella and savory anchovies.*

INGREDIENTS

*1/2 slice white bread, crusts
removed
3 tablespoons milk
1 1/2 pounds ground beef
1 egg, beaten
2/3 cup dry bread crumbs
olive oil for brushing
2 beefsteak or other large
tomatoes, sliced
1 tablespoon chopped fresh
oregano
6 slices mozzarella cheese
6 canned anchovy fillets, drained
and cut in half lengthwise
salt and freshly ground black
pepper*
SERVES 6

1 Put the bread and milk into a small
saucepan and heat very gently, until the
bread absorbs all the milk. Mash it to a
pulp and set aside to cool.

2 Put the ground beef into a bowl
with the bread mixture and the egg and
season with plenty of salt and freshly
ground black pepper. Mix well, then
shape the mixture into 6 patties, using
your hands. Sprinkle the bread crumbs
onto a plate and dredge the patties,
coating them thoroughly.

3 Brush the polpette with olive
oil and cook them on a hot grill for
2–3 minutes on one side, until brown.
Turn them over.

4 Without removing the polpette
from the grill, lay a slice of tomato on
top of each one, sprinkle with chopped
oregano and season with salt and
pepper. Place a mozzarella slice on top
and arrange 2 strips of anchovy in a
cross over the cheese.

5 Cook for another 4–5 minutes,
until the polpette are cooked through
and the mozzarella has melted.

STUFFED KIBBEH

Kibbeh is a tasty Middle Eastern speciality of ground lamb and bulgur, which can be eaten raw or shaped into patties and cooked on the grill.

INGREDIENTS

1 pound lean lamb
3 tablespoons olive oil
avocado slices and fresh cilantro
sprigs, to serve

FOR THE KIBBEH
1 1/3 cups bulgur
1 fresh red chili, seeded and
roughly chopped
1 onion, roughly chopped
salt and freshly ground black
pepper

FOR THE STUFFING
1 onion, finely chopped
2/3 cup pine nuts
2 tablespoons olive oil
1 1/2 teaspoons ground allspice
4 tablespoons chopped fresh
cilantro

SERVES 4–6

1 Roughly cut the lamb into chunks, using a heavy kitchen knife. Process the chunks in a blender or food processor until finely ground. Divide the ground meat into two equal portions and set aside until needed.

2 To make the kibbeh, soak the bulgur in cold water for 15 minutes. Drain well, then process in the blender or food processor with the chopped chili and onion, half the meat and plenty of salt and pepper.

3 To make the stuffing, fry the onion and pine nuts in the olive oil for 5 minutes. Add the allspice and remaining ground meat and fry gently, breaking up the meat with a wooden spoon, until browned. Stir in the cilantro and a little seasoning.

4 Turn the kibbeh mixture out onto a clean work surface and use your hands to shape the mixture into a flat round. Divide into 12 wedges.

5 Flatten a wedge in the palm of your hand and spoon a little stuffing onto the center. Bring the edges of the kibbeh over the stuffing to enclose it. Form into a firm egg-shaped mold between the palms of your hands, making sure that the filling is completely enclosed. Repeat with the other wedges.

6 To grill the kibbeh, lightly brush with olive oil and cook on a medium grill for 10–15 minutes, turning carefully, until evenly browned and cooked through. To fry the kibbeh, heat oil to a depth of 2 inches in a large pan until a few kibbeh crumbs sizzle when dropped on the surface. Lower half the kibbeh into the oil and fry for about 5 minutes, until golden. Drain on paper towels and keep hot while frying the remainder. Serve hot with avocado slices and fresh cilantro sprigs.

HERB POLENTA

*Golden polenta made with fresh summer herbs and served with grilled
tomatoes makes a tasty appetizer or light snack.*

INGREDIENTS

3 cups stock or water
1 teaspoon salt
1 cup polenta
2 tablespoons butter
5 tablespoons mixed chopped fresh
parsley, chives and basil, plus extra
to garnish
olive oil for brushing
4 large plum or beef tomatoes,
halved
salt and freshly ground black
pepper

SERVES 4

1 Prepare the polenta in advance:
Place the stock or water in a saucepan,
with the salt, and bring to a boil.
Reduce the heat and stir in the polenta.

2 Stir constantly over moderate heat
for 5 minutes, until the polenta begins
to thicken and come away from the
sides of the saucepan.

3 Remove from the heat and stir in
the butter, chopped herbs and pepper.

4 Lightly grease a wide pan or dish
and pour the polenta into it, spreading
it evenly. Set aside until cool and set.

5 Turn out the polenta and cut into
squares or stamp out rounds with a
large cookie cutter. Brush with olive oil.
Lightly brush the tomatoes with oil and
sprinkle with salt and pepper. Cook the
tomatoes and polenta on a medium-hot
grill for about 5 minutes, turning once.
Serve garnished with fresh herbs.

Cook's Tip

Try using fresh basil or fresh chives
alone, for a distinctive flavor.

BRIE PARCELS WITH ALMONDS

• • •

Creamy French Brie makes a sophisticated appetizer or light meal, wrapped in grape leaves and served hot with chunks of crusty bread.

2 Cut the Brie into four chunks and place each chunk on a grape leaf.

3 Mix together the chives, ground almonds, peppercorns and olive oil, and place a spoonful on top of each piece of cheese. Sprinkle with sliced almonds.

4 Fold the grape leaves over tightly to enclose the cheese completely. Brush the parcels with olive oil and cook on a hot grill for 3–4 minutes, until the cheese is hot and melting. Serve immediately.

INGREDIENTS

4 large grape leaves, in brine
7-ounce piece Brie cheese
2 tablespoons chopped fresh chives
2 tablespoons ground almonds
1 teaspoon crushed black
peppercorns
1 tablespoon olive oil, plus extra
for brushing
sliced almonds

SERVES 4

1 Rinse the grape leaves thoroughly under cold running water and dry them well. Spread the leaves out on a clean work surface or chopping board.

TOFU STEAKS

∘ ∘ ∘

*Vegetarians and meat-eaters alike will enjoy these barbecued tofu steaks. The combination of
ingredients in the marinade gives the steaks a distinctly Japanese flavor.*

INGREDIENTS

*1 container fresh tofu (4 × 3¼
× 1¼ inches), 11 ounces
drained weight
2 scallions, thinly sliced,
to garnish
mixed salad leaves, to garnish*

FOR THE MARINADE
*3 tablespoons sake
2 tablespoons soy sauce
1 teaspoon sesame oil
1 garlic clove, crushed
1 tablespoon grated fresh ginger
1 scallion, finely chopped*

SERVES 4

1 Wrap the tofu in a clean dish towel
and place it on a chopping board. Put a
large plate on top and let stand for 30
minutes to remove any excess water.

2 Slice the tofu horizontally into
three pieces, then cut the slices into
quarters. Set aside. Mix the ingredients
for the marinade in a large bowl. Add
the tofu to the bowl in a single layer
and allow to marinate for 30 minutes.
Drain the tofu steaks and reserve the
marinade to use for basting.

3 Cook the steaks on the grill for
3 minutes on each side, basting
regularly with the marinade, or fry
them for 3 minutes in a large pan.

4 Arrange 3 tofu steaks on each
plate. Any remaining marinade can be
heated in a pan and then poured over
the steaks. Sprinkle with the scallions
and garnish with mixed salad leaves.
Serve immediately.

Cook's Tip
Tofu is easily obtainable
from supermarkets and health
food stores, and is an ideal
alternative to meat.

GRILLED ASPARAGUS WITH SALT-CURED HAM

○ ○ ○

Grilled asparagus has a wonderfully intense flavor that stands up well to the wrapping of crisp, salty ham. Serve this traditional tapas dish with drinks before a meal.

INGREDIENTS

6 slices of Serrano ham
12 asparagus spears
1 tablespoon olive oil
sea salt and coarsely ground black pepper

SERVES 4

1 Halve each slice of ham lengthwise and wrap one half around each of the asparagus spears.

2 Brush the ham and asparagus lightly with olive oil and sprinkle with salt and pepper. Cook on a medium grill for about 4 minutes, turning frequently, until the asparagus is tender but still firm. Serve at once.

Cook's Tip

If you can't find Serrano ham, try using Italian prosciutto or Portuguese presunto.

POTATO SKINS WITH CAJUN DIP

· · ·

As an alternative to deep-frying, grilling potato skins crisps them up in no time and gives them a wonderful charbroiled flavor. This spicy dip makes the perfect partner.

INGREDIENTS

4 large baking potatoes
olive oil for brushing
1 cup plain yogurt
2 garlic cloves, crushed
2 teaspoons tomato paste
1 teaspoon green chili paste or
1 small green chili, chopped
½ teaspoon celery salt
salt and freshly ground black
pepper

SERVES 4

1 Bake or microwave the potatoes until tender. Cut them in half and scoop out the flesh, leaving a thin layer of flesh on the skins. The scooped-out potato can be reserved in the refrigerator or freezer for another meal.

2 Cut each potato shell in half again and lightly brush the skins with olive oil. Cook on a medium-hot grill for 4–5 minutes, or until crisp.

3 To make the dip, mix together the remaining ingredients in a bowl. Serve the potato skins with the Cajun dip on the side.

Cook's Tip
If you don't have any chili paste or fresh chilies, add one or two drops of hot pepper sauce to the dip instead.

27

SPICY CHICKEN WINGS

These deliciously sticky bites will appeal to adults and children alike, although younger eaters might prefer a little less chili powder.

INGREDIENTS

8 plump chicken wings
2 large garlic cloves, cut into slivers
1 tablespoon olive oil
1 tablespoon paprika
1 teaspoon chili powder
1 teaspoon dried oregano
salt and freshly ground black pepper
lime wedges, to serve

SERVES 4

1 Using a small, sharp kitchen knife, make one or two cuts in the skin of each chicken wing and slide a sliver of garlic under the skin. Brush the wings generously with the olive oil.

2 In a large bowl, stir together the paprika, chili powder and oregano and season with plenty of salt and pepper. Add the chicken wings and toss together until very lightly coated in the mixture.

3 Cook the chicken wings on a medium grill for 15 minutes, until they are cooked through and the skins are blackened and crisp. Serve with fresh lime wedges.

CHICKEN WINGS TERIYAKI STYLE

This Japanese-style glaze is very simple to prepare and adds a unique flavor to the meat.
The glaze can be used with any cut of chicken or with fish.

INGREDIENTS

1 garlic clove, crushed
3 tablespoons soy sauce
2 tablespoons dry sherry
2 teaspoons honey
2 teaspoons grated fresh ginger
1 teaspoon sesame oil
12 chicken wings
1 tablespoon sesame seeds, toasted

SERVES 4

1 Place the garlic, soy sauce, sherry, honey, grated ginger and sesame oil in a large bowl and beat with a fork, to mix the ingredients together evenly.

2 Add the chicken wings and toss thoroughly, to coat in the marinade. Cover the bowl with plastic wrap and chill for 30 minutes or longer.

3 Cook the chicken wings on a fairly hot grill for 20–25 minutes, turning occasionally and basting with the remaining marinade.

4 Sprinkle the chicken wings with sesame seeds. Serve the wings on their own as an appetizer or side dish, or as a light meal with a crisp green salad.

29

SKEWERED LAMB WITH RED ONION SALSA

° ° °

A simple salsa makes a refreshing accompaniment to this summery dish—make sure you use a mild-flavored red onion that is fresh and crisp, and a tomato that is ripe and full of flavor.

INGREDIENTS

8 ounces lean lamb, cubed
½ teaspoon ground cumin
1 teaspoon ground paprika
1 tablespoon olive oil
salt and freshly ground black pepper

FOR THE SALSA
1 red onion, very thinly sliced
1 large tomato, seeded and chopped
1 tablespoon red wine vinegar
3 or 4 fresh basil or mint leaves, roughly torn
small mint leaves, to garnish

SERVES 4

1 Place the lamb in a large bowl with the cumin, paprika and olive oil and season with plenty of salt and freshly ground black pepper. Toss well. Cover the bowl with plastic wrap and let sit in a cool place for several hours or in the refrigerator overnight, so that the lamb fully absorbs the spicy flavors.

2 Spear the lamb cubes on four small skewers. If using wooden skewers, soak them first in cold water for at least 30 minutes to prevent them from burning when placed on the grill.

3 To make the salsa, put the sliced onion, tomato, red wine vinegar and torn fresh basil or mint leaves in a small bowl and stir together until thoroughly blended. Season to taste with salt and garnish with mint.

4 Cook the skewered lamb on a hot grill or under a hot broiler for 5–10 minutes, turning the skewers frequently, until the lamb is well browned but still slightly pink in the center. Serve hot, with the salsa.

SPICY MEATBALLS

o o o

These meatballs are delicious served piping hot with chili sauce. Keep the sauce on the side so that everyone can add as much heat as they like.

2 Add the ground beef, shallots, garlic, bread crumbs, beaten egg and parsley, with plenty of salt and pepper. Mix well, then use your hands to shape the mixture into 18 small balls.

3 Brush the meatballs with olive oil and cook on a medium grill, or fry them in a large pan, for about 10–15 minutes, turning regularly until evenly browned and cooked through.

INGREDIENTS

4 ounces fresh spicy sausages
4 ounces ground beef
2 shallots, finely chopped
2 garlic cloves, finely chopped
1½ cups fresh white bread crumbs
1 egg, beaten
2 tablespoons chopped fresh
parsley, plus extra to garnish
1 tablespoon olive oil
salt and freshly ground black
pepper
Tabasco or other hot chili sauce,
to serve

SERVES 6

1 Use your hands to remove the skins from the sausages, placing the sausage meat in a mixing bowl and breaking it up with a fork.

4 Transfer the meatballs to a warm dish and sprinkle with chopped fresh parsley. Serve with chili sauce.

FIVE-SPICE RIB-STICKERS

. . .

*To make these a real success, choose the meatiest spareribs you can find;
remember to keep a supply of paper napkins within easy reach.*

2 Mix together all the remaining ingredients except the scallions; pour this mixture over the ribs. Toss well to coat evenly. Cover the bowl and let marinate in the refrigerator overnight.

3 Cook the ribs on a medium-hot grill, turning frequently, for 30–40 minutes. Brush occasionally with the remaining marinade.

INGREDIENTS

2¼ pounds Chinese-style pork
spareribs
2 teaspoons Chinese five-spice
powder
2 garlic cloves, crushed
1 tablespoon grated fresh ginger
½ teaspoon chili sauce
4 tablespoons dark soy sauce
3 tablespoons dark brown sugar
1 tablespoon sunflower oil
4 scallions

SERVES 4

1 If the spareribs are still attached to each other, cut between them to separate them (or you could ask your butcher to do this when you buy them). Place the spareribs in a large bowl.

4 While the ribs are cooking, finely slice the scallions. Sprinkle them over the ribs and serve immediately.

SALMON WITH SPICY PESTO

o o o

This is a great way to bone salmon steaks to give a solid piece of fish. The pesto is made with
sunflower or pumpkin seeds and chilies rather than the classic basil and pine nuts.

INGREDIENTS

4 salmon steaks, about
8 ounces each
2 tablespoons sunflower oil
finely grated rind and juice
of 1 lime
salt and freshly ground
black pepper

FOR THE PESTO
6 mild fresh red chilies
2 garlic cloves
2 tablespoons sunflower or
pumpkin seeds
juice and finely grated rind
of 1 lime
5 tablespoons olive oil

SERVES 4

1 Insert a very sharp knife close to
the top of the bone. Working close
to the bone, cut your way to the end
of the steak to release one side. Repeat
with the other side. Pull out any visible
extra bones with a pair of tweezers.

2 Sprinkle salt on a work surface and
take hold of the end of the salmon
piece, skin side down. Insert the knife
between the skin and the flesh and,
working away from you, remove the
skin, keeping the knife as close to it as
possible. Repeat for each piece of fish.

3 Curl each piece of fish into a
round, with the thinner end wrapped
around the fatter end. Secure the shape
tightly with a length of string.

4 Rub the sunflower oil into the
boneless fish rounds. Put the salmon in
a large bowl or dish and add the lime
juice and rind and the salt and pepper.
Allow the salmon to marinate in the
refrigerator for up to 2 hours.

5 For the pesto, seed the chilies and
place, with the garlic cloves, sunflower
or pumpkin seeds, lime juice, rind and
seasoning, in a food processor. Process
until well mixed. With the blades
moving, gradually pour in the olive oil
until the sauce has thickened and
emulsified. Drain the salmon from its
marinade. Cook the fish steaks on a
medium grill for 5 minutes on each side
and serve with the spicy pesto.

GRILLED JUMBO SHRIMP WITH ROMESCO SAUCE

° ° °

This sauce comes from the Catalan region of Spain and is served with fish and seafood.
Its main ingredients are pimiento, tomatoes, garlic and almonds.

INGREDIENTS

24 uncooked jumbo shrimp
2–3 tablespoons olive oil
flat-leaf parsley, to garnish
lemon wedges, to serve

FOR THE SAUCE
2 ripe, flavorful tomatoes
4 tablespoons olive oil
1 onion, chopped
4 garlic cloves, chopped
1 canned pimiento, chopped
1/2 teaspoons crushed red pepper or
chili powder
5 tablespoons fish stock
2 tablespoons white wine
10 blanched almonds
1 tablespoon red wine vinegar
salt

SERVES 4

1 To make the sauce, immerse the tomatoes in boiling water for about 30 seconds, then refresh them under cold running water. Peel away the skins and roughly chop the flesh.

2 Heat 2 tablespoons of the oil. Add the onion and 3 of the garlic cloves; cook until soft. Add the pimiento, tomatoes, crushed red pepper, fish stock and wine. Cover and simmer for 30 minutes.

3 Toast the almonds under the broiler until golden. Transfer to a blender or food processor and grind coarsely. Add the remaining 2 tablespoons oil, the vinegar and the last garlic clove and process until evenly combined. Add the tomato and pimiento sauce and process until smooth. Season with salt.

4 Remove the heads from the shrimp, leaving them otherwise unshelled, and, with a sharp knife, slit each one down the back and remove the dark vein. Rinse and pat dry on paper towels. Toss the shrimp in olive oil, then spread them out on the grill and cook over medium heat for 2–3 minutes on each side, until pink. Serve at once, garnished with parsley and accompanied by lemon wedges and the romesco sauce.

QUICK SEAFOOD PIZZA

· · ·

Make four mini-pizzas or one large one with the same quantities of ingredients.
If you are short of time, use a pizza-crust mix instead of making the dough.

INGREDIENTS

FOR THE PIZZA CRUST
1 teaspoon active dry yeast
4 cups bread flour
1 tablespoon sugar
1 teaspoon sea salt
1¼ cups lukewarm water
2 tablespoons extra virgin olive oil

FOR THE FISH TOPPING
1 tablespoon olive oil
1 onion, finely chopped
1¾ pound canned or fresh plum
tomatoes, chopped
salt and freshly ground black
pepper
1 tablespoon chopped fresh thyme
4 ounces cherry tomatoes, halved
12 fresh anchovy fillets, or 1 can
anchovy fillets, drained
8 fresh, peeled shrimp
a few sprigs of fresh thyme,
to garnish

SERVES 4

1 Stir the yeast into the flour in a large bowl. Add the sugar and sea salt and mix together well.

2 Add the water and olive oil to the bowl, and stir to make a firm dough.

3 Knead the dough for about 10 minutes. Cover and let sit in a warm place until it has doubled in size.

4 Knock back the dough and knead for 5 minutes, then cut the dough into 4 pieces. Shape each of the 4 pieces of dough into a 5-inch round.

5 Fry the onions until soft. Add the tomatoes, seasoning and thyme and simmer for 15 minutes. Brush the pizza dough rounds with olive oil and cook on a medium-hot grill, oiled side down, for 6–8 minutes, until firm and golden underneath. Oil the uncooked side and turn the pizzas over.

6 Cut the cherry tomatoes in half. On each of the pizzas place a spoonful of the sauce, three anchovy fillets, two shrimp and some cherry tomato halves. Return the pizzas to the grill and cook for another 8–10 minutes, until golden and crispy. Sprinkle a few fresh sprigs of thyme on top of the pizzas to serve.

Variation
Add your favorite seafood, such as fresh or canned mussels, to the topping.

MEAT
DISHES

Succulent cuts of meat are often the starting-point when planning

a meal cooked on the grill, and charbroiling gives meat a unique flavor.

A perfect steak or lamb chop, simply seasoned and brushed with oil

before broiling, is utterly delicious. Even ordinary sausages and burgers

for an impromptu family supper can be turned into a treat on the grill.

With a little forethought you can add variety and originality to your

cooking by marinating the meat for a few hours before you cook it.

The simplest marinade will work wonders: improving the texture and

juiciness of the meat as well as adding the flavors of herbs and spices.

The recipes in this chapter draw on cuisines from all over the world to

offer an exciting range of dishes that are all easy to prepare and delicious.

SAUSAGES WITH PRUNES AND BACON

Sausages are a perennial barbecue favorite, and this is a delicious and unusual way to prepare them. Serve with crusty French bread or warmed ciabatta.

2 Spread the cut surface with the mustard and then place 3 prunes in each sausage, pressing them in firmly.

3 Stretch the bacon slices out thinly, using the back of a metal spatula.

4 Wrap one bacon slice tightly around each of the sausages, to hold them in shape. Cook over a hot grill for 15–18 minutes, turning occasionally, until evenly browned and thoroughly cooked. Serve at once, with lots of fresh crusty bread and mustard.

INGREDIENTS

8 large garlic and herb pork
sausages, or other good-quality
meaty sausages
2 tablespoons Dijon mustard,
plus extra to serve
24 pitted prunes
8 slices lean smoked bacon

SERVES 4

1 Use a sharp knife to cut a long slit down the length of each sausage, about three-quarters of the way through.

SHISH KEBAB

. . .

*Many different kinds of kebab are eaten throughout the Middle East, and they are
almost always cooked over an open wood or charcoal fire.*

INGREDIENTS

1 pound boned leg of lamb, cubed
1 large green bell pepper, seeded
and cut into squares
1 large yellow bell pepper, seeded
and cut into squares
8 baby onions, halved
8 ounces button mushrooms
4 tomatoes, halved
1 tablespoons melted butter
bulgur, to serve

FOR THE MARINADE
3 tablespoons olive oil
juice of 1 lemon
2 garlic cloves, crushed
1 large onion, grated
1 tablespoon fresh oregano
salt and freshly ground black
pepper

SERVES 4

3 Cook the kebabs and tomatoes on
a hot grill for 10 minutes, turning
occasionally and basting with butter.
Serve with prepared bulgur.

1 First make the marinade: Blend
together the olive oil, lemon juice,
crushed garlic, onion, fresh oregano
and seasoning. Place the meat in
a shallow dish and pour the marinade
over it. Cover with plastic wrap and
allow to marinate for several hours,
or overnight, in the refrigerator.

2 Thread the lamb onto metal
skewers, alternating with pieces of
pepper, onions and mushrooms. Thread
the tomatoes onto separate skewers.

BACON KOFTA KEBABS AND SALAD

Kofta kebabs can be made with any type of ground meat, but bacon is very successful, if you have a food processor.

INGREDIENTS
9 ounces lean bacon slices, roughly chopped
1 small onion, roughly chopped
1 celery stick, roughly chopped
5 tablespoons fresh whole-wheat bread crumbs
3 tablespoons chopped fresh thyme
2 tablespoons Worcestershire sauce
1 egg, beaten
salt and freshly ground black pepper
olive oil, for brushing

FOR THE SALAD
¾ cup bulgur wheat
4 tablespoons toasted sunflower seeds
1 tablespoon olive oil
salt and freshly ground black pepper
handful of celery leaves, chopped

SERVES 4

1 Place the bacon, onion, celery and bread crumbs in a food processor and process until chopped. Add the thyme, Worcestershire sauce and seasoning. Bind to a firm mixture with the egg.

2 Divide the mixture into 8 equal portions and use your hands to shape them around 8 bamboo skewers.

3 For the salad, place the bulgur in a bowl and pour boiling water over it to cover. Let stand for 30 minutes, until the grains are tender.

4 Drain well, then stir in the sunflower seeds, olive oil, salt and pepper. Stir in the celery leaves.

5 Cook the kofta skewers over a medium-hot grill for 8–10 minutes, turning occasionally, until golden brown. Serve with the salad.

BEEF RIB WITH ONION SAUCE

° ° °

*Rib of beef is a classic large cut for roasting, but just one rib, grilled on the bone, and then
carved into succulent slices, makes a perfect dish for two. Serve with a mellow red onion sauce.*

INGREDIENTS

1 beef rib on the bone, about 2¼
pounds and about 1½ inches
thick, well trimmed of fat
1 teaspoon "steak pepper" or
lightly crushed black peppercorns
1 tablespoon coarse sea salt,
crushed
2–3 tablespoons olive oil

FOR THE RED ONION SAUCE
3 tablespoons butter
1 large red onion or 8–10 shallots,
sliced
1 cup beef or chicken stock
1–2 tablespoons red currant jelly
¼ teaspoon dried thyme
salt and freshly ground black
pepper

SERVES 2

1 Wipe the beef with damp paper
towels. Mix the steak pepper or
crushed peppercorns with the crushed
salt and press onto both sides of the
meat. Let the meat stand, loosely
covered, for 30 minutes.

2 To make the sauce, melt the butter
over medium heat. Add the onion
or shallots and cook for 3 minutes,
until softened. Add the wine, stock,
jelly and thyme and bring to a boil.
Reduce the heat and simmer for
30–35 minutes, until the liquid has
evaporated and the sauce has
thickened. Season and keep warm.

3 Brush the meat with olive oil and
cook on a hot grill, or in a pan over
high heat, for 5–8 minutes on each
side, depending on how rare you like it.
Transfer the beef to a board, cover
loosely and let stand for about 10
minutes. Using a knife, loosen the meat
from the rib bone, then carve into thick
slices. Serve with the onion sauce.

STILTON BURGERS

A variation on the traditional hamburger, this tasty recipe contains a delicious surprise:
a creamy filling of lightly melted Stilton cheese.

INGREDIENTS

1 pound ground beef
1 onion, chopped
1 celery stick, chopped
1 teaspoon dried mixed herbs
1 teaspoon prepared mustard
1/2 cup crumbled Stilton cheese
4 hamburger buns
salt and freshly ground black
pepper
salad and mustard pickle, to serve

SERVES 4

1 Mix the ground beef with the chopped onion, celery, mixed herbs and mustard. Season well with salt and pepper, and bring together with your hands to form a firm mixture.

2 Divide the mixture into 8 equal portions. Shape 4 portions into rounds and flatten each one slightly. Place a little of the crumbled cheese in the center of each round.

3 Shape and flatten the remaining four portions and place on top. Use your hands to mold the rounds together, encasing the crumbled cheese and shaping them into four burgers.

4 Cook on a medium grill for about 10 minutes or until cooked through, turning once. Split the hamburger buns and place a burger inside each one. Serve with salad and mustard pickle.

THAI BEEF SALAD

A hearty salad of beef and crunchy vegetables, laced with a tangy chili and lime dressing. The grilled meat gives the salad a truly delicious flavor.

INGREDIENTS

2 sirloin steaks, about
8 ounces each
1 red onion, finely sliced
1/2 cucumber, sliced into matchsticks
1 stalk lemongrass, finely chopped
2 tablespoons chopped scallions
juice of 2 limes
1–2 tablespoons Thai fish sauce
2–4 red chilies, finely sliced, to
garnish
fresh cilantro, Chinese mustard
cabbage and mint leaves, to
garnish

SERVES 4

1 Grill or pan-fry the beef steaks until they are medium rare. Allow the steaks to rest for 10–15 minutes.

2 When the steaks have cooled slightly, slice them thinly, using a heavy knife, and put the slices into a large bowl.

3 Add the sliced onion, cucumber matchsticks and chopped lemongrass.

4 Add the scallions. Toss and season with lime juice and Thai fish sauce. Serve at room temperature or chilled, garnished with the chilies, cilantro, mustard cabbage and mint.

NEW ORLEANS STEAK SALAD

The New Orleans "poor boy" started life in the Creole community, as a sandwich filled with leftover scraps. This salad, made with tender beef steak, is a variation on the sandwich.

INGREDIENTS

4 sirloin or round steaks,
about 6 ounces each
1 head of escarole
1 bunch of watercress
4 tomatoes, quartered
4 large cornichons, sliced
4 spring onions, sliced
4 canned artichoke hearts, halved
6 ounces button mushrooms, sliced
12 green olives
½ cup French dressing
salt and freshly ground black
pepper

SERVES 4

1 Season the steaks with plenty of black pepper and cook on a hot grill, or under a hot broiler , for 4–6 minutes, turning once, until medium rare. Cover and let the steaks rest in a warm place.

2 Combine the salad leaves with all the ingredients except the steak, and toss with the French dressing.

3 Divide the salad among four plates. Slice each steak diagonally and arrange the slices over the salad. Season with salt and fresh black pepper and serve.

SPICED BEEF SATAY

· ◦ ·

*Tender strips of steak threaded on skewers and spiced with the characteristic flavors
of Indonesia are popular with everyone. Tamarind pulp can be found in Asian markets.*

INGREDIENTS

1 pound sirloin steak, cut into
½-inch strips
1 teaspoon coriander seeds, dry-
fried and ground
½ teaspoon cumin seeds, dry-fried
and ground
1 teaspoon tamarind pulp
1 small onion
2 garlic cloves
1 tablespoon brown sugar
1 tablespoon dark soy sauce
salt

TO SERVE
cucumber chunks
lemon or lime wedges
Sambal Kecap

MAKES 18 SKEWERS

1 Mix the meat and spices in a large
nonmetallic bowl. Soak the tamarind
pulp in ⅓ cup water.

2 Strain the tamarind and reserve the
juice. Put the onion, garlic, tamarind
juice, sugar and soy sauce in a food
processor and blend well.

3 Pour the marinade over the meat
and spices and toss together well. Let
stand for at least 1 hour.

4 Meanwhile, soak some bamboo
skewers in water to prevent them
from burning while cooking. Thread
5 or 6 pieces of meat onto each skewer
and sprinkle with salt. Cook on a hot
grill, turning frequently and basting
with the marinade, until tender.

5 Serve with cucumber chunks and
wedges of lemon or lime for squeezing
over the meat. Sambal Kecap is a
traditional accompaniment.

SAMBAL KECAP
Mix 1 fresh red chili,
seeded and finely chopped,
2 crushed garlic cloves and
4 tablespoons dark soy sauce with
4 teaspoons lemon juice and
2 tablespoons hot water in a
bowl. Let stand for 30 minutes
before serving.

VEGETABLE-STUFFED BEEF ROLLS

These Japanese-style beef rolls are very popular for al fresco meals. You could roll up many other vegetables in the sliced beef. Pork is also very good cooked this way.

INGREDIENTS

2 ounces carrot
2 ounces green pepper, seeded
1 bunch of scallions
14 ounces beef round, thinly sliced
all-purpose flour, for dusting
1 tablespoon olive oil
fresh parsley sprigs, to garnish

FOR THE SAUCE
2 tablespoons sugar
3 tablespoons soy sauce
3 tablespoons mirin

SERVES 4

1 Use a sharp knife to shred the carrot and green pepper into 1½- to 2-inch lengths. Wash and peel the outer skins from the scallions, then halve them lengthwise. Shred the scallions diagonally into 1½- to 2-inch lengths.

2 The beef slices should be cut paper thin and measure about 6 inches square. Lay a slice of beef on a chopping board and top with strips of the carrot, green pepper and scallion. Roll up tightly and dust lightly with flour. Repeat with the remaining beef and vegetables.

3 Secure the beef rolls with toothpicks, soaked in water to prevent them from burning, and cook on a medium grill, or in a pan over medium heat, for 10–15 minutes, turning frequently, until golden brown and thoroughly cooked.

4 Blend the ingredients for the sauce in a small pan and heat to dissolve the sugar and form a glaze. Halve the cooked rolls, cutting at a slant, and stand them on a plate with the sloping cut ends facing upward. Dress with the sauce and garnish with fresh parsley.

LAMB STEAKS MARINATED IN MINT AND SHERRY

*The marinade in this recipe is extremely quick to prepare, and is the key
to its success: the sherry imparts a wonderful tang to the meat.*

INGREDIENTS

*6 large lamb steaks or
12 smaller chops*

FOR THE MARINADE
*2 tablespoons chopped fresh mint
leaves
1 tablespoons black peppercorns
1 medium onion, chopped
$^1/_2$ cup sherry
4 tablespoons extra virgin olive oil
2 garlic cloves*

SERVES 6

1 Finely chop the mint leaves and
peppercorns in a food processor. Add
the onion and process again until
smooth. Add the rest of the marinade
ingredients and process until
completely mixed. The marinade
should have a thick consistency.

2 Add the marinade to the meat and
cover with plastic wrap. Place in the
refrigerator to marinate overnight.

3 Cook the steaks on a medium grill
for 10–15 minutes, basting occasionally
with the marinade.

SKEWERED LAMB WITH CILANTRO YOGURT

These Turkish kebabs are traditionally made with lamb, but lean beef or pork works equally well.
You can alternate pieces of bell pepper, lemon or onions with the meat for extra flavor and color.

INGREDIENTS

2 pounds boneless lean lamb
1 large onion, grated
3 bay leaves
5 sprigs of thyme or rosemary
grated rind and juice of 1 lemon
1/2 teaspoon sugar
1/3 cup olive oil
salt and freshly ground black
pepper
sprigs of fresh rosemary, to garnish
barbecued lemon wedges, to serve

FOR THE CILANTRO YOGURT
2/3 cup thick plain yogurt
1 tablespoon chopped fresh mint
1 tablespoon chopped fresh
cilantro
2 teaspoons grated onion

SERVES 4

1 To make the cilantro yogurt, mix together the yogurt, chopped fresh mint, chopped fresh cilantro and grated onion. Transfer the yogurt to a serving bowl.

2 To make the kebabs, cut the lamb into 1-inch cubes and place in a bowl. Mix together the onion, herbs, lemon rind and juice, sugar and oil, then season to taste.

3 Pour the marinade over the meat in the bowl and stir so that the meat is thoroughly covered. Cover with plastic wrap and marinate in the refrigerator for several hours or overnight.

4 Drain the meat and thread onto metal skewers. Cook on a hot grill for about 10 minutes. Garnish with rosemary and grilled lemon wedges and serve with the cilantro yogurt.

LAMB BURGERS WITH RED CURRANT CHUTNEY

These very special burgers take a little extra time to prepare but are well worth it.
The red currant chutney is the perfect complement to the minty lamb taste.

INGREDIENTS

1¼ pounds ground lean lamb
1 small onion, finely chopped
2 tablespoons finely chopped
fresh mint
2 tablespoons finely chopped
fresh parsley
4 ounces mozzarella cheese
2 tablespoons oil, for basting
salt and freshly ground black
pepper

FOR THE RED CURRANT CHUTNEY
1½ cups fresh or frozen red
currants
2 teaspoons clear honey
1 teaspoon balsamic vinegar
2 tablespoons finely chopped mint

SERVES 4

1 In a large bowl, mix together the ground lamb, chopped onion, mint and parsley until evenly combined. Season well with plenty of salt and freshly ground black pepper.

Cook's Tip

If time is short, or if fresh red currants are not available, serve the burgers with ready-made red currant sauce.

2 Roughly divide the meat mixture into eight equal pieces and use your hands to press each of the pieces into a flat round.

3 Cut the mozzarella into 4 chunks. Place 1 chunk of cheese on half the lamb rounds. Top each one with another round of meat mixture.

4 Press each of the 2 rounds of meat together firmly, making 4 flattish burger shapes. Use your fingers to blend the edges and seal in the cheese completely.

5 Place all the ingredients for the chutney in a bowl and mash them together with a fork. Season well with salt and freshly ground black pepper.

6 Brush the lamb burgers with olive oil and cook them on a moderately hot grill for about 15 minutes, turning once, until golden brown. Serve on hamburger buns with the chutney.

GRILLED LAMB WITH POTATO SLICES

• • •

*A traditional mixture of fresh herbs adds a summery flavor to this simple lamb dish.
The leg of lamb will cook more evenly on the grill if it's boned, or "butterflied," first.*

INGREDIENTS

1 leg of lamb, about 4½ pounds
1 garlic clove, thinly sliced
handful of fresh flat-leaf parsley
handful of fresh sage
handful of fresh rosemary
handful of fresh thyme
6 tablespoons dry sherry
4 tablespoons walnut oil
1¼ pounds medium-size potatoes
salt and freshly ground
black pepper

SERVES 4

2 Use a sharp kitchen knife to scrape away the meat from the bone on both sides, until the bone is completely exposed. Carefully remove the bone and cut away any sinews and excess fat from the meat.

4 Place the meat in a bowl and pour the sherry and walnut oil over it. Chop half the remaining herbs and sprinkle over the meat. Cover the bowl with a clean dish towel and let marinate in the refrigerator for 30 minutes.

1 Place the lamb on a board, smooth side down, so that you can see where the bone lies. Using a sharp, heavy knife, make a long cut through the flesh down to the bone.

3 Cut through the thickest part of the meat so that you can open it out as flat as possible. (Your butcher can butterfly the meat for you if you prefer.) Then make several cuts in the lamb with a sharp kitchen knife, and push slivers of garlic and sprigs of fresh herbs into the cuts.

5 Remove the lamb from the marinade and season it. Cook on a medium-hot grill for 30–35 minutes, turning occasionally and basting with the reserved marinade.

Cook's Tip

If you have a spit-roasting attachment, the lamb can be rolled and tied with herbs inside, and spit roasted for 1–1½ hours. A spit makes it much easier to cook larger pieces of lamb.

6 Scrub the potatoes, then slice them thickly. Brush with the marinade and place around the lamb. Cook for about 15 minutes, until golden brown.

LAMB WITH LAVENDER BALSAMIC MARINADE

° ° °

Lavender is an unusual flavor to use with meat, but its heady, summery scent works well with grilled lamb. If you prefer, rosemary can take its place.

2 Sprinkle the chopped fresh lavender over the lamb in the bowl.

3 Beat together the vinegar, olive oil and lemon juice and pour over the lamb. Season well with salt and pepper, then turn to coat evenly.

INGREDIENTS

4 racks of lamb, with 3–4 cutlets
each
1 shallot, finely chopped
3 tablespoons chopped fresh
lavender
1 tablespoon balsamic vinegar
2 tablespoons olive oil
1 tablespoon lemon juice
salt and freshly ground black
pepper
handful of lavender sprigs

SERVES 4

1 Place the racks of lamb in a large mixing bowl or wide dish and sprinkle the chopped shallot over them.

4 Sprinkle a few lavender sprigs over the broiler or on the coals of a medium-hot grill. Cook the lamb for 15–20 minutes, turning once and basting with any remaining marinade, until golden brown on the outside and still slightly pink in the center.

LAMB WITH MINT AND LEMON

Use this simple and traditional marinade to make the most of fine-quality lamb leg steaks.
Lemon and fresh mint combine extremely well with the flavor of grilled lamb.

INGREDIENTS

4 lamb steaks, about 8 ounces each
fresh mint leaves, to garnish

FOR THE MARINADE
grated rind and juice of ½ lemon
1 garlic clove, crushed
1 scallion, finely chopped
1 teaspoon finely chopped fresh
mint
2 tablespoons extra virgin olive oil
salt and freshly ground black
pepper

SERVES 4

1 Mix all the marinade ingredients and season to taste. Place the lamb steaks in a shallow dish and add the marinade. Cover with plastic wrap and allow to marinate in the refrigerator for several hours or overnight.

2 Drain the lamb from the marinade and cook on a medium-hot grill for 10–15 minutes or until just cooked, basting occasionally with the marinade and turning once. Garnish the lamb steaks with the fresh mint leaves.

STUFFED EGGPLANT WITH LAMB

*Ground lamb and eggplant go together beautifully. This is an attractive dish,
with the different-colored peppers in the lightly spiced stuffing mixture.*

INGREDIENTS

2 medium eggplants
2 tablespoons vegetable oil
1 medium onion, sliced
1 teaspoon grated fresh ginger
1 teaspoon chili powder
1 garlic clove, crushed
¼ teaspoon turmeric
1 teaspoon salt
1 teaspoon ground coriander
1 medium tomato, chopped
12 ounces lean ground lamb
1 medium green bell pepper,
roughly chopped
1 medium orange bell pepper,
roughly chopped
2 tablespoons chopped fresh
cilantro
rice, to serve

FOR THE GARNISH
½ onion, sliced
2 cherry tomatoes, quartered
fresh cilantro sprigs

SERVES 4

1 Cut the eggplants in half
lengthwise with a heavy knife. Scoop
out most of the flesh and reserve it for
another dish. Brush the shells with a
little vegetable oil.

2 In a medium saucepan, heat 1
tablespoon oil and fry the sliced onion
until golden brown. Stir in the grated
ginger, chili powder, garlic, turmeric,
salt and coriander. Add the chopped
tomato, lower the heat and cook for
about 5 minutes, stirring constantly.

3 Add the ground lamb to the
saucepan and continue to cook over
medium heat for 7–10 minutes. Stir
in the chopped fresh peppers and the
fresh cilantro.

4 Spoon the lamb mixture into the
eggplant shells and brush the edges
of the shells with the remaining oil.
Cook on a medium grill for 15–20
minutes, until cooked through. Garnish
with sliced onion, cherry tomatoes and
cilantro, and serve with rice, if desired.

VEAL CHOPS WITH BASIL BUTTER

∘ ∘ ∘

Veal chops from the loin are an expensive cut and are best cooked quickly and simply.
The flavor of basil goes well with veal, but other herbs can be used instead if you prefer.

INGREDIENTS

2 tablespoons butter, softened
1 tablespoon Dijon mustard
1 tablespoon chopped fresh basil
olive oil, for brushing
2 veal loin chops, 1-inch thick,
8 ounces each
salt and freshly ground black
pepper
fresh basil sprigs, to garnish

SERVES 2

1 To make the basil butter, cream the softened butter with the Dijon mustard and chopped fresh basil in a large mixing bowl, then season with plenty of freshly ground black pepper.

2 Brush both sides of each chop with olive oil and season with a little salt.

3 Cook the chops on a hot grill for 7–10 minutes, basting with oil and turning once, until done to your liking. (Medium-rare meat will still be slightly soft when pressed, medium meat will be springy, and well-done firm.) Top each chop with half the basil butter and serve at once, garnished with basil.

67

LEMONGRASS PORK CHOPS WITH MUSHROOMS

Thai flavorings are used to make an aromatic marinade and a spicy sauce. The sauce can be put together in a pan on the grill while the chops and mushrooms are cooking.

INGREDIENTS
4 pork chops, about 8 ounces each
4 large field mushrooms
3 tablespoons vegetable oil
4 fresh red chilies, seeded and
finely sliced
3 tablespoons Thai fish sauce
6 tablespoons lime juice
4 shallots, chopped
1 teaspoon roasted ground rice
2 tablespoons chopped scallions
fresh cilantro leaves,
to garnish
4 scallions, shredded,
to garnish

FOR THE MARINADE
2 garlic cloves, chopped
1 tablespoon sugar
1 tablespoon Thai fish sauce
2 tablespoons soy sauce
1 tablespoon sesame oil
1 tablespoon whiskey or dry sherry
2 stalks lemongrass, finely
chopped
2 scallions, chopped

SERVES 4

2 Place the mushrooms and marinated pork chops on a rack and brush with 1 tablespoon vegetable oil. On a medium-hot grill, cook the pork chops for 10–15 minutes and the mushrooms for about 2 minutes, turning once. Brush both with the marinade while cooking.

3 Meanwhile, heat the remaining oil in a small frying pan, then remove from the heat and mix in the remaining ingredients. Put the pork chops and mushrooms on a serving plate and spoon the sauce over them. Garnish with the fresh cilantro leaves and shredded scallions.

1 To make the marinade, mix all the ingredients. Arrange the pork chops in a shallow dish. Pour the marinade over them and let sit for 1–2 hours.

FARMHOUSE PIZZA

° ° °

Pizza is not a dish usually associated with barbecue cooking, but in fact the open fire
gives the crust a wonderfully crisp texture. Shape the dough to fit the rack of your grill.

INGREDIENTS

6 tablespoons olive oil
8 ounces button mushrooms,
sliced
11-ounce package pizza-crust mix
1¼ cups tomato sauce
11 ounces mozzarella cheese, thinly
sliced
4 ounces wafer-thin slices
smoked ham
6 bottled artichoke hearts in oil,
drained and sliced
2-ounce can anchovy fillets,
drained and halved lengthwise
10 pitted black olives, halved
2 tablespoons chopped fresh
oregano
3 tablespoons freshly grated
Parmesan cheese
freshly ground black pepper

SERVES 8

1 Heat 2 tablespoons oil in a pan, add the mushrooms and fry until all the juices have evaporated. Let cool.

2 Make up the pizza dough according to the directions on the package. Roll it out on a floured surface to a 12 × 10-inch rectangle. Brush with oil and place, oiled side down, on a medium-hot grill. Cook for 6 minutes, until firm.

3 Brush the uncooked side of the dough with oil and turn over. Spread with the tomato sauce and arrange the sliced mozzarella on top. Scrunch up the smoked ham and arrange on top of the pizza with the artichoke hearts, anchovies and cooked mushrooms.

4 Dot with the halved olives, then sprinkle with the fresh oregano and Parmesan. Drizzle with the remaining olive oil and season with black pepper. Return to the grill and cook for another 8–10 minutes, or until the dough is golden brown and crisp.

POULTRY
AND GAME

⟹⋙⟸

Chicken cooked on the grill is unfailingly popular with both adults
and children, and it can be as simple or sophisticated as you choose:
it is very versatile and takes on a whole range of flavors with great
success. Buy breast fillets to make delicious kebabs and salads with a
minimum of preparation, or cook drumsticks and thighs with robust
spicy coatings. Whole birds can be roasted very effectively on a spit,
or they can be flattened out by removing the backbone and cooked on
the grill rack. It is vital to make sure chicken is always very thoroughly
cooked – it needs a medium heat to cook it through without charring
the outside. Don't forget other types of poultry, particularly duck,
which stays beautifully juicy and moist when cooked on the grill.

CHICKEN WITH PINEAPPLE

The pineapple juice in this Indian recipe is used to tenderize the meat, but it also gives the chicken a deliciously tangy sweetness.

INGREDIENTS

*18-ounce can pineapple chunks
in juice
1 teaspoon ground cumin
1 teaspoon ground coriander
1 garlic clove, crushed
1 teaspoon chili powder
1 teaspoon salt
2 tablespoons low-fat plain yogurt
1 tablespoon chopped fresh cilantro
few drops orange food coloring
(optional)
10 ounces skinned, boned chicken
breast and thigh meat, about 2 cups
½ red bell pepper
½ yellow or green bell pepper
1 large onion
6 cherry tomatoes
1 tablespoon vegetable oil
salad or rice, to serve*

SERVES 6

1 Drain the canned pineapple into a bowl. Reserve 12 large chunks of pineapple. Squeeze the juice from the remaining chunks into the bowl, then discard the chunks. You should be left with about ½ cup pineapple juice.

2 In a large bowl, blend together the cumin, ground coriander, garlic, chili powder, salt, yogurt, fresh cilantro and food coloring, if using. Pour in the pineapple juice and mix together.

3 Cut the chicken into cubes, add to the yogurt and spice mixture and set aside to marinate for 1–1½ hours. Cut the peppers and onion into chunks.

4 Arrange the chicken pieces, vegetables and reserved pineapple chunks alternately on 6 skewers.

5 Brush the kebabs with oil and cook on a medium grill for about 10 minutes, turning regularly and basting the chicken pieces regularly with the marinade, until cooked through. Serve with salad or plain cooked rice.

BLACKENED CAJUN CHICKEN AND CORN

This is a classic Deep South method of cooking in a spiced coating, which can be used for poultry, meat or fish. The coating should begin to char and blacken slightly at the edges.

INGREDIENTS

8 chicken joints (drumsticks, thighs or wings)
2 ears of fresh corn
2 teaspoons garlic salt
2 teaspoons ground black pepper
1½ teaspoons ground cumin
1½ teaspoons paprika
1 teaspoon cayenne pepper
3 tablespoons melted butter
chopped parsley, to garnish

SERVES 4

1 Trim any excess fat from the chicken, but leave the skin in place. Slash the thickest parts with a knife, to allow the flavors to penetrate the meat as much as possible.

2 Pull the husks and silks off the ears of corn, then rinse them under cold running water and pat them dry with paper towels. Cut into thick slices, using a heavy kitchen knife.

3 Mix together all the spices. Brush the chicken and corn with the melted butter and sprinkle the spices over them. Toss well to coat evenly.

4 Cook the chicken pieces on a medium-hot grill for about 25 minutes, turning occasionally. Add the corn after 15 minutes and grill, turning often, until golden brown. Serve garnished with chopped parsley.

CHICKEN WITH HERB AND RICOTTA STUFFING

° ° °

*These little chicken drumsticks are full of flavor, and the stuffing and bacon help to
keep them moist and tender.*

INGREDIENTS

4 tablespoons ricotta cheese
1 garlic clove, crushed
3 tablespoons mixed chopped fresh
herbs, such as chives, flat-leaf
parsley and mint
2 tablespoons fresh brown
bread crumbs
8 chicken drumsticks
8 slices lean smoked bacon
1 teaspoon whole-grain mustard
1 tablespoon sunflower oil
salt and freshly ground black
pepper

SERVES 4

1 Mix together the ricotta, garlic,
herbs and bread crumbs. Season well
with plenty of salt and pepper.

2 Carefully loosen the skin from each
drumstick and spoon a little of the herb
stuffing underneath, smoothing the skin
back over firmly.

3 Wrap a bacon slice tightly around
the wide end of each drumstick, to
hold the skin in place over the stuffing
during cooking.

4 Mix together the mustard and oil
and brush them over the chicken. Cook
on a medium-hot grill for about 25
minutes, turning occasionally.

BABY CHICKENS WITH LIME AND CHILI

Poussins are small birds that are ideal for one to two portions. The best way to prepare them is spatchcocked—split and flattened out—to ensure more even cooking.

INGREDIENTS

4 poussins or Cornish game hens,
about 1 pound each
3 tablespoons butter
2 tablespoons sun-dried tomato
paste
finely grated rind of 1 lime
2 teaspoons chili sauce
juice of ½ lime
lime wedges, to serve
fresh flat leaf parsley sprigs,
to garnish

SERVES 4

2 Turn the poussin over and, with poultry shears or strong kitchen scissors, cut down either side of the backbone. Remove it and discard.

3 Turn the poussin breast side up and flatten it gently. Lift the breast skin carefully and gently ease your fingertips underneath, to loosen it from the flesh.

4 Mix together the butter, sun-dried tomato paste, lime rind and chili sauce in a small bowl. Spread about three-quarters of the mixture under the skin of the poussins, smoothing it evenly over the surface of the flesh.

5 To hold the poussins flat during cooking, thread two skewers through each bird, crossing at the center. Each skewer should pass through a drumstick and then out through a wing on the other side.

6 Mix the reserved paste with the lime juice and brush it over the skin of the poussins. Cook on a medium-hot grill, turning occasionally, for 25–30 minutes, or until there is no trace of pink in the juices when the flesh is pierced. Garnish with lime wedges and fresh flat leaf parsley.

1 Place each poussin or hen on a chopping board, breast side upward, and press down firmly with your hand, to break the breastbone.

CHICKEN COOKED IN SPICES AND COCONUT

． ． ．

This chicken dish can be prepared in advance until you are ready to light the grill. Serve it with naan (a flat, leavened Indian bread). Creamed coconut can be found in Asian markets.

INGREDIENTS

7-ounce block creamed
coconut
1¼ cups boiling water
3 garlic cloves, chopped
2 scallions, chopped
1 fresh green chili, chopped
2-inch piece fresh ginger,
chopped
1 teaspoon fennel seeds
½ teaspoon black peppercorns
seeds from 4 cardamom pods
2 tablespoons ground coriander
1 teaspoon ground cumin
1 teaspoon ground star anise
1 teaspoon ground nutmeg
½ teaspoon ground cloves
½ teaspoon ground turmeric
4 large chicken breasts, skinned
and boned
onion rings and fresh cilantro
sprigs, to garnish

SERVES 4

2 Make several diagonal cuts across the chicken breasts. Arrange in a layer in a shallow dish. Spoon on half the coconut mixture and toss well to coat evenly. Cover the dish and let the chicken marinate for at least 30 minutes, or overnight in the refrigerator.

3 Cook the chicken on a medium grill for 12–15 minutes, turning once, until well browned and thoroughly cooked. Heat the remaining coconut mixture gently until boiling. Serve with the chicken, garnished with onion rings and sprigs of cilantro.

1 Break up the coconut and put it in a bowl. Pour the boiling water over it and set aside to dissolve. Place the chopped garlic, scallions, chili, ginger and all of the spices in a blender or food processor. Pour in the coconut mixture and blend to a smooth paste.

GRILLED CASHEW CHICKEN

∘ ∘ ∘

This dish comes from the beautiful Indonesian island of Bali, where nuts are widely used as a base for sauces and marinades. Serve it with a green salad and a hot chili dipping sauce.

INGREDIENTS

4 chicken legs
radishes, sliced, to garnish
½ cucumber, sliced, to garnish
Chinese cabbage, to serve

FOR THE MARINADE
2 ounces raw cashew or macadamia nuts
2 shallots, or 1 small onion, finely chopped
2 garlic cloves, crushed
2 small red chilies, chopped
2-inch piece lemongrass
1 tablespoon tamarind sauce
2 tablespoons dark soy sauce
1 tablespoon Thai fish sauce
2 teaspoons sugar
½ teaspoon salt
1 tablespoon rice or white wine vinegar

SERVES 4

1 Using a sharp kitchen knife, slash the chicken legs several times through to the bone. Chop off the knuckle end and discard.

2 To make the marinade, place the cashew or macadamia nuts in a food processor and grind until fine (or use a pestle and mortar to grind them).

3 Add the chopped shallots or onion, garlic, chilies and lemongrass and blend. Add the remaining marinade ingredients and blend again.

4 Spread the marinade over the chicken and leave for up to 8 hours in the refrigerator. Cook the chicken on a medium grill for 25 minutes, basting and turning occasionally. Garnish with radishes and cucumber and serve on a bed of Chinese cabbage.

HOT AND SOUR CHICKEN SALAD

*This chicken salad from Vietnam is equally delicious made with shrimp.
Allow one pound of fresh shrimp tails to serve four people.*

INGREDIENTS

*2 chicken breasts, skinned and
boned
4 ounces bean sprouts
1 head Chinese cabbage, shredded
2 medium carrots, cut into
matchsticks
1 red onion, thinly sliced
2 large gherkins, sliced*

FOR THE MARINADE
*1 small red chili, seeded and finely
chopped
1/2-in piece fresh ginger, chopped
1 garlic clove, crushed
1 tablespoon crunchy peanut
butter
2 tablespoons chopped fresh
cilantro
1 teaspoon sugar
1/2 teaspoon salt
1 tablespoon rice or white wine
vinegar
4 tablespoons vegetable oil
2 teaspoons Thai fish sauce*

SERVES 4–6

1 Slice the chicken breasts thinly and place in a shallow bowl. Grind the chili, ginger and garlic in a food processor (or grind using a mortar and pestle), then add the peanut butter, chopped fresh cilantro, sugar and salt.

2 Add the rice or white wine vinegar, 2 tablespoons of the oil and the fish sauce to the ingredients in the food processor. Combine well. Cover the chicken with the spice mixture and let it marinate for at least 2–3 hours.

3 Cook the chicken on a medium-hot grill or in a frying pan on the stove for about 5 minutes, basting often and turning once. Arrange the salad ingredients on a serving dish and top with the cooked chicken.

CHICKEN SALAD WITH LAVENDER AND HERBS

The delightful scent of lavender has a natural affinity with garlic, orange, and fresh herbs. The addition of fried polenta makes this salad filling as well as delicious.

INGREDIENTS

4 boneless chicken breasts
3¾ cups light chicken stock
1 cup fine polenta or cornmeal
4 tablespoons butter, plus extra for greasing
1 pound young spinach
6 ounces lamb's lettuce
8 sprigs fresh lavender
8 small tomatoes, halved
salt and freshly ground black pepper

FOR THE MARINADE
6 fresh lavender flowers
2 teaspoons finely grated orange zest
2 garlic cloves, crushed
2 teaspoons clear honey
2 tablespoons olive oil
2 teaspoons chopped fresh thyme
2 teaspoons chopped fresh marjoram
salt

SERVES 4

1 To make the marinade, strip the lavender flowers from the stems and combine with the orange zest, garlic, honey and salt. Add the oil and herbs. Slash the chicken deeply, spread the mixture over it and let it marinate in the refrigerator for 20 minutes.

2 To make the polenta, bring the chicken stock to a boil in a heavy saucepan. Add the cornmeal in a steady stream, stirring all the time, until thick. Turn the cooked polenta out onto a shallow buttered platter and let it cool.

3 Cook the chicken on a medium grill or under the broiler for about 15 minutes, basting with the marinade and turning once, until cooked through.

4 Cut the polenta into 1-inch cubes using a wet knife. Heat the butter in a large frying pan and fry the polenta until golden.

5 Divide the salad leaves between four dinner plates. Slice each chicken breast and arrange over the salad. Arrange the polenta among the salad, decorate with sprigs of lavender and tomato halves, season with salt and freshly ground black pepper and serve.

THAI GRILLED CHICKEN

Thai grilled chicken is especially delicious when cooked outdoors on the barbecue.
Serve it on a bed of crisp salad with lime wedges to offset its richness.

INGREDIENTS

2 pounds chicken drumsticks or
thighs
salt and freshly ground
black pepper
crisp lettuce leaves, to serve
½ cucumber, cut into strips,
to garnish
4 scallions, trimmed,
to garnish
2 limes, quartered, to garnish

FOR THE MARINADE
1 teaspoon black peppercorns
½ teaspoon caraway or cumin
seeds
4 teaspoons sugar
2 teaspoons paprika
¾-inch piece fresh ginger, chopped
3 garlic cloves, crushed
1 tablespoon finely chopped fresh
cilantro, white root or stem
3 tablespoons vegetable oil

SERVES 4–6

1 Chop through the narrow end of each drumstick with a heavy knife. Score the chicken pieces deeply to allow the marinade to penetrate and arrange in a shallow bowl.

2 Grind the peppercorns, caraway or cumin seeds and sugar with a mortar and pestle or in a food processor. Add the paprika, ginger, garlic, cilantro and oil and grind to a paste.

3 Spread the marinade over the chicken and let marinate in the refrigerator for 6 hours. Cook the chicken on a medium grill for about 20 minutes, basting with the marinade and turning once. Season, arrange on a bed of lettuce and garnish before serving.

MEDITERRANEAN TURKEY SKEWERS

*These attractive kebabs can be assembled in advance and left to marinate until you are ready
to cook them. Grilling intensifies the Mediterranean flavors of the vegetables.*

INGREDIENTS

2 medium zucchini
1 long thin eggplant
*11 ounces boneless turkey, cut
into 2-inch cubes*
12–16 pearl onions
*1 red or yellow bell pepper, cut
into 2-inch squares*

FOR THE MARINADE
6 tablespoons olive oil
3 tablespoons fresh lemon juice
1 garlic clove, finely chopped
2 tablespoons chopped fresh basil
*salt and freshly ground black
pepper*

SERVES 4

3 Prepare the skewers by alternating
the turkey, onions and pepper pieces.
Lay the prepared skewers on a platter
and sprinkle with the flavored oil.
Allow to marinate for 30 minutes.

4 Cook on a medium grill or
under a broiler, turning the skewers
occasionally, for about 10 minutes,
or until the turkey is cooked and the
vegetables are tender.

1 To make the marinade, mix the
olive oil with the lemon juice, garlic
and chopped fresh basil. Season well
with plenty of salt and black pepper.

2 Slice the zucchini and eggplant
lengthwise into strips ¼ inch thick. Cut
them crosswise about two-thirds down
their length. Discard the shorter
lengths. Wrap half the turkey pieces
with the zucchini slices and the other
half with the eggplant slices.

PHEASANT WITH SAGE AND LEMON

○ ○ ○

Pheasant is quick to cook and makes a very special summer meal.
This recipe can also be used for guinea fowl.

INGREDIENTS

2 pheasant, about 1 pound each
1 lemon
4 tablespoons chopped fresh sage
3 shallots
1 teaspoon Dijon mustard
1 tablespoon brandy or dry sherry
1²/3 cup crème fraîche
salt and freshly ground black
pepper
lemon wedges and sage sprigs, to
garnish

SERVES 4

2 Finely grate the rind from half the lemon and slice the rest thinly. Mix together the lemon rind and half the chopped sage in a small bowl.

3 Loosen the skin on the breasts and legs of the pheasant and push a little of the sage mixture underneath. Tuck the lemon slices under the skin, smoothing the skin back firmly.

4 Place the half pheasants on a medium-hot grill and cook for 25–30 minutes, turning once.

5 Meanwhile, cook the shallots on the grill for 10–12 minutes, turning occasionally, until the skin is blackened and the inside very soft. Peel off the skins, chop the flesh roughly and mash it with the Dijon mustard and brandy or sherry.

6 Stir in the crème fraîche and add the reserved chopped sage. Season with plenty of salt and freshly ground black pepper. Serve the dressing with the pheasant, garnished with lemon wedges and sprigs of fresh sage.

1 Place the pheasant, breast side up, on a chopping board and cut them in half lengthwise, using poultry shears or a sharp kitchen knife.

Cook's Tip
Try to choose pheasant with undamaged skins, so that the flavorings stay in place during cooking.

SPICED DUCK WITH PEARS

∘ ∘ ∘

This delicious casserole can be cooked on the grill or the stove. The browned pears are added toward the end of cooking, along with a pine nut and garlic paste to flavor and thicken.

INGREDIENTS

6 duck portions, either breast or
leg pieces
1 tablespoon olive oil
1 large onion, thinly sliced
1 cinnamon stick, halved
2 thyme sprigs
2 cups duck or chicken stock
mashed potato and green vegetable
(optional), to serve

TO FINISH

3 firm ripe pears, peeled and cored
2 tablespoons olive oil
2 garlic cloves, sliced
1/3 cup pine nuts
1/2 teaspoon saffron strands
2 tablespoons raisins
salt and freshly ground black pepper
thyme sprigs or parsley, to garnish

SERVES 6

1 Fry the duck portions in olive oil for 5 minutes, until golden, or brush the portions with oil and cook them on a hot grill for 8–10 minutes. Transfer the duck to a large flameproof dish. If frying, drain off all but 1 tablespoon of the fat left in the pan.

2 Fry the onion in the frying pan for 5 minutes, until golden. Add the cinnamon stick, thyme and stock and bring to a boil. Pour over the duck in the dish and cook slowly on a low grill for about 1 hour and 15 minutes.

3 Halve the pears, brush with oil and grill until brown, or fry them in the oil on the stove. Pound the garlic, pine nuts and saffron with a mortar and pestle, to make a thick, smooth paste.

4 Add the paste, raisins and pears to the flameproof dish. Cook for 15 minutes, until the pears are tender.

5 Season to taste and garnish with the fresh herbs. Serve with mashed potatoes and a green vegetable, if desired.

Cook's Tip

A good stock is essential for this dish. Buy a large duck (plus two extra duck breasts if you want portions to be generous) and joint it yourself, using the giblets and carcass for stock. If you buy duck portions, use a flavorful chicken stock.

DUCK BREASTS WITH RED PEPPER JELLY GLAZE

° ° °

Sweet potatoes have pinkish skins and flesh varying from creamy white to deep orange.
Choose a long, cylindrical tuber to make neat round slices for this Cajun dish.

INGREDIENTS

2 duck breasts
1 sweet potato, about 14 ounces
2 tablespoons red pepper jelly
1 tablespoon sherry vinegar
4 tablespoons butter, melted
coarse sea salt and freshly ground
black pepper

SERVES 2

4 Meanwhile, warm the red pepper jelly and sherry vinegar together in a bowl set over a saucepan of hot water, stirring to mix them as the jelly melts. Brush the skin of the duck with this jelly glaze and return to the grill, skin side down, for another 2–3 minutes to caramelize it.

5 Brush the sweet potato slices with melted butter and sprinkle with coarse sea salt. Cook on a hot grill for 8–10 minutes, until soft, brushing with more butter and sprinkling with salt and pepper when you turn them. Serve the duck sliced with the sweet potatoes and accompany with a green salad.

1 Slash the skin of the duck breasts diagonally at 1-inch intervals and rub plenty of salt and pepper over the skin and into the cuts.

2 Scrub the sweet potato and cut into ½-inch slices, discarding the ends.

3 Cook the duck breasts on a medium grill, skin side down, for 5 minutes. Turn and cook for another 8–10 minutes, according to how pink you like your duck.

DUCK BREASTS WITH RED PLUMS

The rich fruity sauce for this dish combines brandy and red plums with heavy cream and cilantro. The sauce can be made in a pan on the grill while the duck is cooking.

INGREDIENTS

4 duck breasts, about 6 ounces each, skinned
2 teaspoons crushed cinnamon stick
4 tablespoons butter
1 tablespoon plum brandy or cognac
1 cup chicken stock
1 cup heavy cream
6 fresh red plums, pitted and sliced
6 sprigs fresh cilantro leaves, plus extra to garnish
salt and freshly ground black pepper

SERVES 4

1 Score the duck breasts and sprinkle with salt. Press the crushed cinnamon onto both sides of the duck breasts. Brush with butter and cook on a medium grill for 15–20 minutes, turning once, until the duck is tender.

2 To make the sauce, melt half the remaining butter in a saucepan. Add the brandy or cognac and set it alight. When the flames have died down, add the stock and cream and allow to simmer gently until reduced and thickened. Add seasoning to taste.

3 In a saucepan, melt the other half of the butter and fry the plums with the cilantro just enough to cook the fruit through. Slice the duck breasts and pour some sauce around each one, then garnish with the plum slices and the chopped fresh cilantro.

FISH AND SEAFOOD

———⇒◆⇐———

Cooking over charcoal adds a marvellous flavor to fish and seafood, and it's very quick and easy to prepare this way. Oily fish such as mackerel, sardines or tuna are perfectly suited to broiling and won't dry out, while charbroiling will enhance their robust flavors. Use plump shrimps or firm meaty-textured fish such as monkfish or swordfish for kebabs, but marinate them first to keep them moist. More delicate fish, or those that are best cooked in their own steam, can also be grilled very successfully: just wrap them securely in aluminum foil and cook them either on the rack or directly on the coals. You can include all kinds of flavorings in the foil parcels, too.

Mackerel Kebabs with Sweet Pepper Salad

• • •

Mackerel is an excellent fish for grilling because its natural oils keep it moist and tasty.
This recipe combines mackerel with peppers and tomatoes in a flavorful summer salad.

INGREDIENTS

4 medium mackerel, about
8 ounces each, filleted
2 small red onions, cut into wedges
2 tablespoons chopped fresh
marjoram
4 tablespoons dry white wine
3 tablespoons olive oil
juice of 1 lime

FOR THE SALAD
1 red bell pepper
1 yellow bell pepper
1 small red onion
2 large plum tomatoes
1 tablespoon chopped fresh
marjoram
2 teaspoons balsamic vinegar
salt and freshly ground black
pepper

SERVES 4

1 Thread each mackerel fillet onto a skewer, with an onion wedge on each end. Arrange the skewers in a dish.

2 Mix together the marjoram, wine, oil and lime juice and spoon over the fish. Cover and chill in the refrigerator for at least 30 minutes, turning once.

3 To make the salad, quarter and seed both peppers and halve the onion. Place the peppers and onion, skin side down, with the whole tomatoes on a hot grill and cook until the skins are blackened and charred.

4 Remove the vegetables from the grill and set aside until they are cool enough to handle. Use a sharp knife to peel off and discard the skins.

5 Chop the vegetables roughly and put them in a bowl. Stir in the marjoram and balsamic vinegar and season to taste. Toss thoroughly.

6 Remove the kebabs from the refrigerator and cook on a hot grill for 10–12 minutes, turning occasionally and basting with the marinade. Serve with the pepper salad.

Cook's Tip
Other oily fish can be used for this dish: try fillets or cubes of herring, rainbow trout or salmon, instead.

GRILLED SCALLOPS WITH LIME BUTTER

• • •

Fresh scallops cook quickly, so they're ideal for barbecues. This recipe combines them simply with lime and fennel.

INGREDIENTS

1 fennel bulb
2 limes
12 large scallops, cleaned
1 egg yolk
6 tablespoons melted butter
olive oil for brushing
salt and freshly ground
black pepper

SERVES 4

3 Place the egg yolk and remaining lime rind and juice in a small bowl and whisk until pale and smooth.

5 Brush the fennel wedges with olive oil and cook them on a hot grill for 3–4 minutes, turning once.

1 Trim any feathery leaves from the fennel and reserve them. Slice the bulb lengthwise into thin wedges.

4 Gradually whisk in the melted butter and continue whisking until thick and smooth. Finely chop the reserved fennel leaves and stir them in, with seasoning to taste.

6 Add the scallops and cook for another 3–4 minutes, turning once. Serve with the lime and fennel butter and the lime wedges.

2 Cut one lime into wedges. Finely grate the rind and squeeze the juice from the other lime; toss half the juice and rind with the scallops. Season well with salt and fresh black pepper.

Cook's Tip
If the scallops are small, you may wish to thread them onto flat skewers to make turning them easier.

MONKFISH WITH PEPPERED CITRUS MARINADE
. . .

Monkfish is a firm, meaty fish that keeps its shape well when cooked on the grill.
Serve with a green salad.

INGREDIENTS

2 monkfish tails, about
12 ounces each
1 lime
1 lemon
2 oranges
handful of fresh thyme sprigs
2 tablespoons olive oil
1 tablespoon mixed peppercorns,
roughly crushed
salt and freshly ground
black pepper

SERVES 4

2 Turn the fish and repeat on the other side, to remove the second fillet. Repeat on the second tail. (If you prefer, you can ask your fishmonger to do this for you.) Lay the 4 fillets out flat on a chopping board.

5 Squeeze the juice from the citrus fruits and mix it with the olive oil and more salt and pepper. Spoon over the fish. Cover with plastic wrap and marinate in the refrigerator for about 1 hour, turning occasionally and spooning the marinade over the fish.

1 Using a sharp kitchen knife, remove any skin from the monkfish tails. Cut carefully down one side of the backbone, sliding the knife between the bone and the flesh, to remove the fillet on one side.

3 Cut two slices from each of the citrus fruits and arrange them over 2 of the fillets. Add a few sprigs of fresh thyme and sprinkle with plenty of salt and freshly ground black pepper. Finely grate the rind from the remaining fruit and sprinkle it over the fish.

6 Drain the monkfish, reserving the marinade, and sprinkle with the crushed peppercorns. Cook on a medium-hot grill for 15–20 minutes, basting with the marinade and turning occasionally, until the fish is evenly cooked. Serve immediately.

4 Lay the other 2 fillets on top and tie them firmly at intervals.

GRILLED SNAPPER WITH HOT MANGO SALSA

A ripe mango provides the basis for a deliciously rich fruity salsa that needs no oil and features the tropical flavors of cilantro, ginger and chilies.

INGREDIENTS

12 ounces new potatoes
3 eggs
4 ounces young green beans,
trimmed and halved
4 red snapper, about 12 ounces
each, cleaned, scaled and gutted
2 tablespoons olive oil, plus extra
for brushing
6 ounces mixed lettuce leaves
2 cherry tomatoes
salt and freshly ground black
pepper

FOR THE SALSA
3 tablespoons chopped fresh cilantro
1 medium-size ripe mango, peeled,
pitted and diced
1/2 fresh red chili, seeded and
chopped
1-inch piece fresh ginger, grated
juice of 2 limes
generous pinch of celery salt

SERVES 4

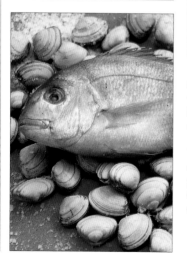

1 Place the potatoes in a large saucepan of salted water. Bring to a boil and simmer for 15–20 minutes· drain.

2 Bring a second large saucepan of salted water to a boil. Put in the eggs and boil for 4 minutes, then add the beans and cook for another 6 minutes, so that the eggs have had a total of 10 minutes. Remove the eggs from the saucepan. Drain and refresh the beans. Cool, then shell the eggs and cut into quarters.

3 Using a sharp knife, slash each snapper 3 times on each side. Brush with olive oil and cook on a medium-hot grill for 12 minutes, basting occasionally and turning once.

4 To make the salsa, place the chopped fresh cilantro in a food processor. Add the mango chunks, chili, grated ginger, lime juice and celery salt and process until smooth.

5 Dress the lettuce leaves with olive oil and distribute them evenly among four large plates.

6 Arrange the snapper on the lettuce and season to taste. Halve the new potatoes and distribute them with the beans, tomatoes and quartered hard-boiled eggs over the salad. Serve immediately, with the salsa.

Variation
If fresh mangoes are unavailable, use canned ones, draining well. Sea bream are also good served with this hot mango salsa.

SMOKED HADDOCK WITH QUICK PARSLEY SAUCE

· · ·

Make any herb sauce by this method, making sure it is thickened and seasoned well to complement the smoky flavor of the fish.

INGREDIENTS

4 smoked haddock fillets, about 8 ounces each
6 tablespoons butter, softened
2 tablespoons all-purpose flour
1¼ cups milk
4 tablespoons chopped fresh parsley
salt and freshly ground black pepper

SERVES 4

1 Smear the fish fillets on both sides with 4 tablespoons of the butter.

2 Beat the remaining butter and the flour together to make a paste.

3 Cook the fish on a medium-hot grill for about 10 minutes, turning once. Meanwhile, to make the sauce, heat the milk in a saucepan to just below boiling point. Add the flour mixture in small spoonfuls, whisking constantly over the heat. Continue until the sauce is smooth and thick.

4 Add the seasoning and chopped fresh parsley to the saucepan and stir well. Pour the parsley sauce over the haddock fillets to serve.

SALMON WITH RED ONION MARMALADE
. . .

Salmon grills well but is most successful when it is at least an inch thick. The red onion marmalade is rich and delicious. Puréed black currants work as well as crème de cassis.

INGREDIENTS
4 salmon steaks, about 6 ounces each
2 tablespoons olive oil
salt and freshly ground black pepper

FOR THE RED ONION MARMALADE
5 medium red onions, peeled and finely sliced
4 tablespoons butter
3/4 cup red wine vinegar
1/4 cup crème de cassis
1/4 cup grenadine
1/4 cup red wine

SERVES 4

1 Use your hands to rub the olive oil into the salmon flesh and season with plenty of salt and freshly ground black pepper.

2 Melt the butter in a large, heavy saucepan and add the sliced onions. Sauté the onions for 5 minutes, until golden brown.

3 Stir in the vinegar, crème de cassis, grenadine and wine and continue to cook for about 10 minutes, until the liquid has almost entirely evaporated and the onions are glazed. Season well.

4 Brush the fish with a little more oil and cook on a medium grill for 6–8 minutes, turning once.

SALMON WITH TROPICAL FRUIT SALSA

Fresh salmon really needs little adornment, but it does combine very well with the exotic flavors in this colorful salsa.

INGREDIENTS

4 salmon steaks or fillets, about 6
ounces each
finely grated rind and juice of
1 lime
1 small, ripe mango
1 small, ripe papaya
1 fresh red chili
3 tablespoons chopped fresh
cilantro
salt and freshly ground black
pepper

SERVES 4

3 Halve the papaya, scoop out the seeds with a spoon and remove the peel. Finely chop the flesh and add it to the mango in the bowl.

4 Cut the chili in half lengthwise. Leave the seeds in to make the salsa hot and spicy, or remove them for a milder flavor. Finely chop the chili.

5 Combine the mango, papaya, chili and cilantro in a bowl and stir in the remaining lime rind and juice. Season to taste with plenty of salt and freshly ground black pepper.

6 Cook the salmon on a medium grill for 5–8 minutes, turning once. Serve with the fruit salsa.

1 Place the salmon in a wide dish and sprinkle with half the lime rind and juice. Season with salt and pepper.

2 Cut the mango in half, cutting along each side of the pit; remove the pit. Finely chop the mango flesh and place it in a bowl.

VEGETARIAN DISHES AND VEGETABLES

Vegetables cooked on the grill acquire a richness and depth of flavor that will add an extra dimension to your meal. There are lots of ideas here for vegetable accompaniments to meat and fish dishes, as well as for substantial main dishes that everyone, vegetarian or not, will love. All vegetables can be cooked in aluminum foil parcels, but many are ideally suited to cooking on the grill: jacket potatoes, bell peppers, eggplant and corn on the cob are irresistible cooked over charcoal, or you can spear a mixture of vegetables onto skewers to make colorful and delicious kebabs. Charbroiled vegetables can also be cooled and made into fabulous salads. They certainly shouldn't be an afterthought on your barbecue menu.

RED BEAN AND MUSHROOM BURGERS

° ° °

Vegetarians, vegans and meat-eaters alike will enjoy these healthy, low-fat veggie burgers.
With salad, pita bread and thick, creamy plain yogurt, they make a substantial meal.

INGREDIENTS

1 tablespoon olive oil
1 small onion, finely chopped
1 garlic clove, crushed
1 teaspoon ground cumin
1 teaspoon ground coriander
1/2 teaspoon ground turmeric
1 1/2 cups finely chopped
mushrooms
14-ounce can red kidney beans
2 tablespoons chopped fresh
cilantro
whole-wheat flour (optional)
olive oil, for brushing
salt and freshly ground black pepper
strained plain yogurt and
green salad, to serve

SERVES 4

1 Heat the olive oil in a frying pan and fry the chopped onion and garlic over moderate heat, stirring, until softened. Add the spices and cook for a minute more, stirring constantly.

Cook's Tip

These burgers are not quite as firm as hamburgers, and will need careful handling on the grill.

2 Add the chopped mushrooms and cook, stirring, until softened and dry. Remove the pan from the heat and empty the contents into a large bowl.

3 Drain the beans thoroughly, place them in a bowl and mash with a fork.

4 Stir the kidney beans into the frying pan, with the chopped fresh cilantro, and mix thoroughly. Season the mixture with plenty of salt and freshly ground black pepper.

5 Using floured hands, form the mixture into 4 flat burger shapes. If the mixture is too sticky to handle, mix in a little whole-wheat flour.

6 Lightly brush the burgers with olive oil and cook on a hot grill for 8–10 minutes, turning once, until golden brown. Serve with a spoonful of yogurt and a green salad, if desired.

GRILLED GOAT CHEESE PIZZA

· · ·

*Pizzas cooked on the grill have a beautifully crisp and golden crust. The combination
of goat cheese and red onion in this recipe makes for a flavorful main course dish.*

2 Brush the dough round with olive oil and place, oiled side down, on a medium grill. Cook for 6–8 minutes, until firm and golden underneath. Brush the uncooked side with olive oil and turn the pizza over.

3 Mix together the tomato sauce and pesto and quickly spread over the cooked side of the pizza, to within about ½ inch of the edge. Arrange the onion, tomatoes and cheese on top and sprinkle with salt and pepper.

INGREDIENTS

5-ounce package pizza-dough mix
olive oil, for brushing
⅔ cup tomato sauce
2 tablespoons tomato pesto
1 small red onion, thinly sliced
8 cherry tomatoes, halved
4 ounces firm goat cheese, thinly
sliced
handful shredded fresh basil leaves
salt and freshly ground black
pepper

SERVES 4

1 Make up the pizza dough according to the directions on the package. Roll out the dough on a lightly floured surface to a round about 10 inches in diameter.

4 Cook the pizza for 10 minutes more, until golden brown and crisp. Sprinkle with fresh basil and serve.

RED ONION GALETTES

° ° °

If non-vegetarians are going to eat these pretty puff pastry tarts, you can sprinkle some chopped anchovies over them before grilling to add extra piquancy.

INGREDIENTS

4–5 tablespoons olive oil
1¼ pounds red onions, sliced
1 garlic clove, crushed
2 tablespoons chopped fresh mixed herbs, such as thyme, parsley and basil
8 ounces ready-made puff pastry
1 tablespoon sun-dried tomato paste
freshly ground black pepper
fresh thyme sprigs, to garnish

SERVES 4

1 Heat 2 tablespoons oil in a frying pan and add the onions and garlic. Cover and cook gently for 15–20 minutes, stirring occasionally, until soft but not browned. Stir in the herbs.

2 Divide the pastry into 4 pieces and roll out each piece to a 6-inch round. Flute the edges, prick all over with a fork and place on baking sheets.

3 Chill the rounds, on the baking sheets, in the refrigerator for 10 minutes. Mix 1 tablespoon of the olive oil with the sun-dried tomato paste and spread over the pastry rounds, to within about ½ inch of the edge.

4 Spread the onion mixture over the pastry and season with pepper. Drizzle with a little oil, then place the baking sheets on a medium grill for 15 minutes, until the pastry is crisp. Serve hot, garnished with thyme sprigs.

143

TOFU SATAY

Grill cubes of tofu until crisp, then serve with a Thai-style peanut sauce. Soak the satay sticks before use to prevent them from burning while on the grill.

INGREDIENTS

7-ounce package smoked tofu
3 tablespoons light soy sauce
2 teaspoons sesame oil
1 garlic clove, crushed
1 yellow and 1 red bell pepper, cut into squares
8–12 fresh bay leaves
sunflower oil, for brushing

FOR THE PEANUT SAUCE
2 scallions, finely chopped
2 garlic cloves, crushed
generous pinch of chili powder, or a few drops of hot chili sauce
1 teaspoon sugar
1 tablespoon white wine vinegar
2 tablespoons light soy sauce
3 tablespoons crunchy peanut butter

SERVES 4–6

1 Cut the tofu into bite-size cubes and place in a large bowl. Add the soy sauce, sesame oil and crushed garlic and mix well. Cover with plastic wrap and marinate for at least 20 minutes.

2 Using a wooden spoon, beat all the peanut sauce ingredients together in a large bowl. Do not use a food processor to blend the ingredients, as the texture should be slightly chunky.

3 Drain the tofu and thread the cubes onto 8–12 satay sticks, alternating the tofu with the bell pepper squares and bay leaves. Larger bay leaves may need to be halved before threading.

4 Brush the satays with sunflower oil and cook on a hot grill or under the broiler, turning occasionally, until the tofu and peppers are browned and crisp. Serve hot with the peanut sauce.

SWEET AND SOUR VEGETABLES WITH PANEER

∘ ∘ ∘

The Indian cheese used in this recipe, called paneer, can be bought at Asian stores, or you can use tofu in its place. Paneer has a good firm texture and cooks very well on the grill.

INGREDIENTS

1 green and 1 yellow bell pepper,
cut into squares
8 cherry, or 4 medium, tomatoes
8 cauliflower florets
8 fresh or canned pineapple chunks
8 cubes paneer

FOR THE SEASONED OIL
1 tablespoon soybean oil
2 tablespoons lemon juice
1 teaspoon salt
1 teaspoon freshly ground black
pepper
1 tablespoon honey
2 tablespoons chili sauce

SERVES 4

1 Thread the prepared vegetables, pineapple and paneer cubes onto 4 skewers, alternating the ingredients.

2 Mix together all the ingredients for the seasoned oil. If the mixture seems a little too thick, add 1 tablespoon water. Brush the vegetables with the seasoned oil.

3 Cook on a hot grill or under the broiler for 10 minutes, turning the skewers often and basting with the seasoned oil. Sprinkle with pepper and serve on a bed of plain boiled rice.

VEGETABLE KEBABS WITH PEPPERCORN SAUCE

⋄ ⋄ ⋄

*Vegetables invariably taste good when cooked on the grill. You can include other
vegetables in these kebabs, depending on what is available at the time.*

INGREDIENTS

24 mushrooms
16 cherry tomatoes
16 large fresh basil leaves
2 zucchini, cut into 16 thick slices
16 large fresh mint leaves
1 large red bell pepper, cut into
16 squares

TO BASTE

8 tablespoons (1 stick) melted
butter
1 garlic clove, crushed
1 tablespoon crushed green
peppercorns
salt

FOR THE GREEN PEPPERCORN SAUCE

4 tablespoons butter
3 tablespoons brandy
1 cup heavy cream
1 teaspoon crushed green
peppercorns

SERVES 4

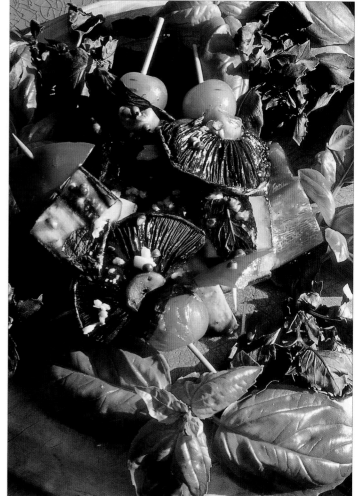

1 Thread the vegetables and herbs
onto 8 bamboo skewers that have been
soaked in water to prevent them from
burning: Place the fresh basil leaves
next to the tomatoes, and wrap the
mint leaves around the zucchini slices.

2 Mix the basting ingredients in a
bowl and baste the kebabs thoroughly.
Cook the skewers on a medium-hot
grill, turning and basting regularly,
until the vegetables are just cooked—
this should take 5–7 minutes.

3 Heat the butter for the green
peppercorn sauce in a frying pan,
then add the brandy and light it. When
the flames have died down, stir in the
cream and the peppercorns. Cook for
2 minutes, stirring constantly. Serve the
sauce with the grilled kebabs.

CASSAVA AND VEGETABLE KEBABS

This is an attractive and delicious assortment of African vegetables, marinated in a spicy garlic sauce, then roasted over hot coals. If cassava is unavailable, use sweet potato or yam instead.

INGREDIENTS

6 ounces cassava
1 onion, cut into wedges
1 eggplant, cut into bite-size pieces
1 zucchini, sliced
1 ripe plantain, sliced
1/2 red bell pepper and 1/2 green
bell pepper, sliced
16 cherry tomatoes
rice or couscous, to serve

FOR THE MARINADE
4 tablespoons lemon juice
4 tablespoons olive oil
3–4 tablespoons soy sauce
1 tablespoon tomato paste
1 green chili, seeded and finely
chopped
1/2 onion, grated
2 garlic cloves, crushed
1 teaspoon apple pie spice
pinch of dried thyme

SERVES 4

1 Peel the cassava and cut into bite-size pieces. Place in a large bowl, cover with boiling water and let it blanch for about 5 minutes. Drain well.

2 Place all the vegetables, including the cassava but not the tomatoes, in a large bowl and mix with your hands so that they are evenly distributed.

3 Blend the marinade ingredients in a bowl and pour over the vegetables. Cover and let marinate for 1–2 hours.

4 Thread the vegetables, with the cherry tomatoes, onto 8 skewers and cook on a hot grill for about 15 minutes, until tender and browned. Turn the skewers frequently and baste them occasionally with the marinade.

5 Pour the remaining marinade into a small saucepan and simmer for about 10 minutes to reduce. Strain the reduced marinade into a bowl. Serve the kebabs on a bed of rice or couscous, with the sauce on the side.

BAKED SQUASH WITH PARMESAN

• • •

Almost all types of squash are suitable for grilling, and they are extremely easy to deal with:
Simply wrap them in aluminum foil and place them in the hot embers until they soften.

INGREDIENTS

2 acorn or butternut squash,
about 1 pound each
1 tablespoon olive oil
4 tablespoons butter, melted
1 cup grated Parmesan cheese
4 tablespoons pine nuts, toasted
salt and freshly ground black
pepper
½ teaspoon freshly grated
nutmeg

SERVES 4

1 Cut the squash in half and scoop out the seeds with a spoon.

2 Brush the cut surfaces with oil and sprinkle with salt and black pepper.

3 Wrap each squash in foil and place in the embers of the fire. Cook for 25–30 minutes, until tender. Turn the parcels occasionally so that the squash cook evenly.

4 When they are cool enough to handle, unwrap the squash from the foil parcels and scoop out the flesh, leaving the skins intact.

5 Dice the flesh, then stir in the melted butter. Add the Parmesan, pine nuts, salt and pepper. Toss well to mix.

6 Spoon the mixture back into the shells. Sprinkle with nutmeg to serve.

Cook's Tip
Spaghetti squash can also be cooked in this way. Just scoop out the spaghetti-like strands and toss with butter and Parmesan cheese.

POTATO AND CHEESE POLPETTE

These little morsels of potato and Greek feta cheese, flavored with dill and lemon juice,
are excellent when grilled, or they can be tossed in flour and fried in olive oil.

INGREDIENTS

1¼ pounds potatoes
4 ounces feta cheese
4 scallions, chopped
3 tablespoons chopped fresh dill
1 egg, beaten
1 tablespoon lemon juice
2 tablespoons olive oil
salt and freshly ground black
pepper

SERVES 4

1 Boil the potatoes in their skins in salted water until soft. Drain, then peel while still warm. Place in a bowl and mash. Crumble the feta cheese into the potatoes and add the scallions, dill, egg and lemon juice and season with pepper and a little salt. Stir well.

2 Cover the mixture and chill until firm. Divide the mixture into walnut-size balls, then flatten them slightly. Brush lightly with olive oil. Arrange the polpette on a grill rack and cook on a medium grill, turning once, until golden brown. Serve at once.

LOOFAH AND EGGPLANT RATATOUILLE

° ° °

Loofahs are edible gourds with spongy, creamy-white flesh. Their flavor, like that of eggplant, is intensified by roasting. Cooking the vegetables in a pan on the grill preserves their juices.

INGREDIENTS

1 large or 2 medium eggplants
1 pound young loofahs, or sponge gourds
1 large red bell pepper, cut into large chunks
8 ounces cherry tomatoes
8 ounces shallots
2 teaspoons ground coriander
4 tablespoons olive oil
2 garlic cloves, finely chopped
a few fresh cilantro sprigs
salt and freshly ground black pepper

SERVES 4

1 Cut the eggplants into thick chunks and sprinkle the pieces liberally with salt to draw out the bitter juices. Allow to drain for about 45 minutes, then rinse under cold running water and pat dry with paper towels.

2 Slice the loofahs into ¾-inch pieces. Place the eggplant, loofah and pepper pieces, together with the cherry tomatoes and shallots, in a roasting pan large enough to hold all the vegetables in a single layer.

3 Sprinkle the vegetables with the ground coriander and olive oil. Sprinkle the chopped garlic and fresh cilantro leaves on top and season to taste.

4 Cook on the grill for about 25 minutes, stirring the vegetables occasionally, until the loofah is golden and the peppers are beginning to char. As an alternative, you could thread the vegetables on skewers and broil them.

151

BAKED STUFFED ZUCCHINI

* * *

The tangy goat cheese stuffing contrasts well with the very delicate flavor of the zucchini in this recipe. Wrap the zucchini in aluminum foil and bake them in the embers of the fire.

2 Insert pieces of goat cheese into the slits. Add a little chopped mint and sprinkle with the oil and black pepper.

3 Wrap each zucchini in foil, place in the embers of the fire and bake for about 25 minutes, until tender.

INGREDIENTS

8 small zucchini, about
1 pound total weight
1 tablespoon olive oil, plus
extra for brushing
3–4 ounces goat cheese,
cut into thin strips
a few sprigs of fresh mint,
finely chopped, plus extra
to garnish
freshly ground black pepper

SERVES 4

1 Cut 8 pieces of aluminum foil large enough to encase each zucchini and lightly brush with olive oil. Trim the zucchini and cut a thin slit along the length of each.

Cook's Tip

While almost any cheese can be used in this recipe, mild cheeses, such as Cheddar or mozzarella, will best allow the flavor of the zucchini to be appreciated.

VEGETABLE PARCELS WITH FLOWERY BUTTER

• • •

Nasturtium leaves and flowers are edible and have a distinctive peppery flavor.
They make a pretty addition to a summer barbecue.

INGREDIENTS

7 ounces baby carrots
9 ounces yellow pattypan squash
or summer squash
4 ounces baby corn
1 onion, thinly sliced
4 tablespoons butter, plus extra
for greasing
finely grated rind of ½ lemon
6 young nasturtium leaves
4–8 nasturtium flowers
salt and freshly ground
black pepper

SERVES 4

1 Trim the vegetables with a sharp knife, leaving them whole unless they are very large—if necessary, cut them into even-size pieces.

2 Divide the vegetables among 4 double-thickness squares of buttered aluminum foil and season well.

3 Mix the butter with the lemon rind in a small bowl. Roughly chop the nasturtium leaves and add them to the butter. Place a generous spoonful of the butter on each pile of vegetables in the squares of foil.

4 Fold over the foil and seal the edges to make a neat parcel. Cook on a medium-hot grill for 30 minutes, until the vegetables are tender. Open the parcels and top each with one or two nasturtium flowers. Serve at once.

GRILLED EGGPLANT PARCELS

These little bundles of tomatoes, mozzarella cheese and basil, wrapped in slices of eggplant, taste delicious cooked on the grill.

INGREDIENTS

2 large, long eggplants
8 ounces mozzarella cheese
2 plum tomatoes
16 large fresh basil leaves
2 tablespoons olive oil
salt and freshly ground black pepper

FOR THE DRESSING
4 tablespoons olive oil
1 teaspoon balsamic vinegar
1 tablespoon sun-dried tomato paste
1 tablespoon lemon juice

FOR THE GARNISH
2 tablespoons toasted pine nuts
torn fresh basil leaves

SERVES 4

1 Remove the stalks from the eggplants and cut them lengthwise into thin slices using a mandoline or long-bladed knife—aim to get 16 slices total, each about ¼ inch thick, not counting the first and last slices.

2 Bring a large saucepan of salted water to the boil and cook the eggplant slices for about 2 minutes, until just softened. Drain the slices, then pat them dry on paper towels.

3 Cut the mozzarella cheese into 8 slices. Cut each tomato into 8 slices, not counting the first and last slices. Take 2 eggplant slices and arrange in a cross. Place a slice of tomato in the center, season, then add a basil leaf, followed by a slice of mozzarella, another basil leaf, another slice of tomato and more seasoning.

4 Fold the ends of the eggplant slices around the filling to make a neat parcel. Repeat with the rest of the assembled ingredients to make 8 parcels. Chill the parcels in the refrigerator for about 20 minutes.

5 To make the tomato dressing, whisk together the olive oil, vinegar, sun-dried tomato paste and lemon juice. Season to taste with plenty of salt and freshly ground black pepper.

6 Brush the parcels with olive oil and cook on a hot grill for about 10 minutes, turning once, until golden. Serve hot, with the dressing, sprinkled with pine nuts and basil.

STUFFED TOMATOES AND PEPPERS

. . .

Colorful peppers and tomatoes make perfect containers for meat and vegetable stuffings. The grilled flavors in this dish are simply superb.

INGREDIENTS

2 large ripe tomatoes
1 green bell pepper
1 yellow or orange bell pepper
4 tablespoons olive oil, plus extra
for sprinkling
2 onions, chopped
2 garlic cloves, crushed
1/2 cup blanched almonds, chopped
scant 1/2 cup long-grain rice, boiled
and drained
2 tablespoons roughly chopped
fresh mint
2 tablespoons roughly chopped
fresh parsley,
2 tablespoons golden raisins
3 tablespoons ground almonds
salt and freshly ground black
pepper
chopped mixed fresh herbs,
to garnish

SERVES 4

2 Halve the peppers, leaving the cores intact. Scoop out the seeds. Brush the peppers with 1 tablespoon olive oil and cook on a medium grill for 15 minutes. Place the peppers and tomatoes on a grill rack and season well with salt and pepper.

3 Fry the onions in the remaining olive oil for 5 minutes. Add the crushed garlic and chopped almonds to the pan and fry for a minute more.

4 Remove the pan from the heat and stir in the rice, chopped tomatoes, mint, parsley and golden raisins. Season well with salt and pepper and spoon the mixture into the tomatoes and peppers.

1 Cut the tomatoes in half and scoop out the pulp and seeds, using a teaspoon. Leave the tomatoes to drain on paper towels with the cut sides facing down. Roughly chop the tomato pulp and set it aside.

5 Sprinkle with the ground almonds and a little extra olive oil. Cook on a medium grill for about 15 minutes. Garnish with fresh herbs.

COUSCOUS-STUFFED PEPPERS

Couscous makes a good basis for a stuffing, and in this recipe it is studded with raisins and flavored with fresh mint. Charred peppers make the combination of flavors truly special.

2 To cook the couscous, bring 1 cup water to a boil. Add the oil and salt, then remove from the heat and add the couscous. Stir and let stand, covered, for 5 minutes. Stir in the onion, raisins and mint. Season well and stir in the egg yolk.

3 Use a teaspoon to fill the peppers with the couscous mixture to about three-quarters full (the couscous will swell while cooking). Wrap each pepper in a piece of oiled aluminum foil.

4 Cook on a medium grill for 20 minutes, until tender. Serve hot or cool, garnished with mint leaves.

INGREDIENTS

6 red bell peppers
2 tablespoons butter
1 onion, finely chopped
1 teaspoon olive oil
$1/2$ teaspoon salt
1 cup couscous
2 tablespoons raisins
2 tablespoons chopped fresh mint
1 egg yolk
salt and freshly ground black pepper
mint leaves, to garnish

SERVES 4

1 Carefully slit each pepper with a sharp knife and remove the core and seeds. Melt the butter in a small saucepan and add the chopped onion. Cook until soft but not browned.

CORN ON THE COB IN A GARLIC BUTTER CRUST

• • •

*Whether you are catering for vegetarians or serving this with meat dishes, it will disappear
in a flash. The charred garlic butter crust adds a new dimension to the corn.*

INGREDIENTS

6 ears of fresh corn
½ pound (2 sticks) butter
2 tablespoons olive oil
2 garlic cloves, crushed
1 cup whole-wheat bread crumbs
1 tablespoon chopped fresh
parsley
salt and freshly ground black
pepper

SERVES 6

1 Pull off the husks and silks and cook the corn in a large saucepan of boiling salted water until tender. Drain and set aside to cool.

2 Melt the butter in a saucepan, add the olive oil, crushed garlic, salt and freshly ground black pepper, and stir to blend. Pour the mixture into a shallow dish. In another shallow dish blend the bread crumbs and chopped fresh parsley. Roll the corn in the melted butter mixture and then in the bread crumbs until they are well coated.

3 Cook the corn on a hot grill for about 10 minutes, turning frequently, until the bread crumbs are golden brown.

STUFFED PARSLEYED ONIONS

* * *

These stuffed onions are a popular vegetarian dish served with fresh crusty bread and a crisp salad. They also make a very good accompaniment to meat dishes.

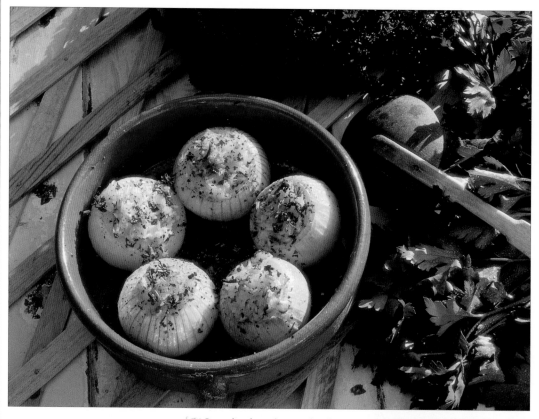

INGREDIENTS

4 large onions
4 tablespoons cooked rice
4 teaspoons finely chopped fresh parsley, plus extra to garnish
4 tablespoons finely grated sharp Cheddar cheese
2 tablespoons olive oil
1 tablespoon white wine
salt and freshly ground black pepper

SERVES 4

1 Cut a slice from the top of each onion and scoop out the center, leaving a fairly thick shell. Combine all the remaining ingredients in a large bowl and stir to mix, moistening with enough white wine to bind the ingredients together well.

2 Use a spoon to fill the onions, then wrap each one in a piece of oiled aluminum foil. Bake in the embers of the fire for 30–40 minutes, until tender, turning the parcels often so they cook evenly. Serve the onions garnished with chopped fresh parsley.

160

STUFFED ARTICHOKE BOTTOMS

The distinctive flavor of charbroiled globe artichokes is matched in this dish by an intensely savory stuffing of mushrooms, cheese and walnuts.

INGREDIENTS

8 ounces button mushrooms
1 tablespoon butter
2 shallots, finely chopped
2 ounces full- or medium-fat soft
cheese, such as ricotta
2 tablespoons chopped walnuts
3 tablespoons grated Gruyère
4 large or 6 small artichoke
bottoms (from cooked artichokes,
leaves and choke removed, or
cooked frozen or canned artichoke
hearts)
salt and freshly ground black
pepper
fresh parsley sprigs, to garnish

SERVES 4

1 To make the duxelles for the stuffing, put the mushrooms in a food processor or blender and pulse until finely chopped.

2 Melt the butter in a frying pan and cook the shallots over medium heat for 2–3 minutes, until just softened. Add the mushrooms, raise the heat slightly, and cook for 5–7 minutes more, stirring frequently, until all the liquid from the mushrooms has been driven off and they are almost dry. Season with plenty of salt and freshly ground black pepper.

3 In a large bowl, combine the soft cheese and cooked mushrooms. Add the chopped walnuts and half the grated Gruyère, and stir well to combine the mixture.

4 Arrange the artichoke bottoms in an oiled baking pan; divide the stuffing mixture among them. Sprinkle with the remaining grated cheese. Grill for 12 minutes, garnish with parsley and serve.

SPINACH WITH RAISINS AND PINE NUTS

• • •

Raisins and pine nuts are frequent partners in Spanish dishes. In this recipe, they are tossed with wilted spinach and croutons; the mixture can be cooked quickly in a flameproof pan on the grill.

INGREDIENTS

1/3 cup raisins
1 thick slice crusty white bread
3 tablespoons olive oil
1/3 cup pine nuts
1 1/4 pounds young spinach, stalks removed
2 garlic cloves, crushed
salt and freshly ground black pepper

SERVES 4

1 Put the raisins in a bowl, cover with boiling water and let soak for 10 minutes. Drain and set aside.

2 Cut the bread into cubes and discard the crusts. Heat 2 tablespoons of the olive oil in a large frying pan and fry the bread until golden brown.

3 Heat the remaining oil and fry the pine nuts, on the grill or stove, until beginning to color. Add the spinach and garlic and cook quickly, turning the spinach until it has just wilted. Toss in the raisins and season lightly with salt and pepper. Transfer to a serving dish. Scatter with croutons and serve.

GRILLED VEGETABLE TERRINE

A colorful layered terrine, using all the vegetables associated with the Mediterranean, makes a successful and elegant dish for outdoor eating. Grilling the vegetables adds to the flavor.

INGREDIENTS

2 large red bell peppers,
quartered, cored and seeded
2 large yellow bell peppers,
quartered, cored and seeded
1 large eggplant, sliced
lengthwise
2 large zucchini, sliced
lengthwise
6 tablespoons olive oil
1 large red onion, thinly sliced
½ cup raisins
1 tablespoon tomato paste
1 tablespoon red wine vinegar
1⅔ cups tomato juice
2 tablespoons powdered gelatin
fresh basil leaves, to garnish

FOR THE DRESSING
6 tablespoons extra virgin olive oil
2 tablespoons red wine vinegar
salt and freshly ground black
pepper

SERVES 6

1 Cook the peppers, skin side down, on a hot grill or under the broiler, until the skins are beginning to blacken. Transfer to a bowl, cover and let cool.

2 Brush the eggplant and zucchini slices with oil and cook until tender and golden, turning occasionally.

3 Heat the remaining oil in a pan and add the onion, raisins, tomato paste and red wine vinegar. Cook until soft and syrupy. Allow to cool in the pan.

4 Pour half the tomato juice into a saucepan and sprinkle with the gelatin. Dissolve gently over very low heat, stirring constantly.

5 Line an oiled 7½-cup terrine with plastic wrap, leaving a little hanging over the sides. Place a layer of red peppers in the bottom and pour in enough of the tomato juice with gelatin to cover. Repeat with the eggplant, zucchini, yellow peppers and onion mixture, ending with another layer of red peppers and covering each layer with tomato juice and gelatin.

6 Add the remaining tomato juice to any left in the pan and pour into the terrine. Give it a sharp tap to eliminate air bubbles. Cover the terrine with plastic wrap and chill until set.

7 To make the dressing, whisk the oil and vinegar, and season with salt and black pepper. Turn out the terrine and serve in thick slices, drizzled with the dressing. Garnish with the basil leaves.

163

SUMMER VEGETABLES WITH YOGURT PESTO

*Grilled vegetables make a meal on their own, or are delicious served as a
Mediterranean-style accompaniment to grilled meats and fish.*

INGREDIENTS

2 small eggplants
2 large zucchini
1 red bell pepper
1 yellow bell pepper
1 fennel bulb
1 red onion
olive oil, for brushing
salt and freshly ground black
pepper

FOR THE YOGURT PESTO
2/3 cup strained plain yogurt
3 tablespoons pesto

SERVES 4

1 Cut the eggplants into ½-inch slices. Sprinkle with salt and let drain for about 30 minutes. Rinse well in cold running water and pat dry.

2 Use a sharp kitchen knife to cut the zucchini in half lengthwise. Cut the peppers in half, removing the seeds but leaving the stalks in place.

3 Slice the fennel bulb and the red onion into thick wedges, using a sharp kitchen knife.

4 Stir the yogurt and pesto lightly together in a bowl, to make a marbled sauce. Spoon the yogurt pesto into a serving bowl and set aside.

5 Arrange the vegetables on the hot grill, brush generously with olive oil and sprinkle with plenty of salt and freshly ground black pepper.

6 Cook the vegetables until golden brown and tender, turning occasionally. The eggplants and peppers will take 6–8 minutes to cook, the zucchini, onion and fennel 4–5 minutes. Serve the vegetables as soon as they are cooked, with the yogurt pesto.

Cook's Tip
Baby vegetables make excellent candidates for grilling whole; look for baby eggplants and peppers, in particular. There's no need to salt the eggplants if they're small.

POTATO WEDGES WITH GARLIC AND ROSEMARY

° ° °

Toss the potato wedges in fragrant, garlicky olive oil with chopped fresh rosemary,
before grilling them over the coals.

INGREDIENTS

1¹/₂ pounds medium potatoes
1 tablespoon olive oil
2 garlic cloves, thinly sliced
4 tablespoons chopped fresh
rosemary
salt and freshly ground black
pepper

SERVES 4

1 Cut each potato into 4 wedges and parboil in boiling salted water for 5 minutes. Drain well.

2 Toss the potatoes in the olive oil with the garlic, rosemary and black pepper. Arrange on a grill rack.

3 Cook the potatoes on a hot grill for about 15 minutes, turning occasionally, until crisp and golden brown.

168

SPANISH POTATOES

This is an adaptation of a traditional recipe for peppery fried potatoes. Cook the potatoes in a flameproof dish on the grill or in a pan on the stove, and serve them with grilled meats.

INGREDIENTS

1½ pounds small new potatoes
5 tablespoons olive oil
2 garlic cloves, sliced
½ teaspoon crushed red pepper
½ teaspoon ground cumin
2 teaspoons paprika
2 tablespoons red or white wine vinegar
1 red or green bell pepper, sliced
coarse sea salt, to serve (optional)

SERVES 4

1 Cook the potatoes in a saucepan of boiling salted water until almost tender. Drain and cut into chunks.

2 Heat the olive oil in a large frying pan or sauté pan and fry the potatoes, turning them frequently, until golden.

3 Meanwhile, crush the garlic, crushed red pepper and cumin in a mortar and pestle. Mix with the paprika and vinegar to form a thick paste.

4 Add the garlic mixture to the potatoes with the sliced bell pepper and cook, stirring, for 2 minutes. Serve warm or let sit until cool. Sprinkle with coarse sea salt, if you wish, to serve.

SALADS AND ACCOMPANIMENTS

———◆———

Cool salads are a perfect foil to grilled food, but they should

have assertive characters of their own. The recipes that follow

include some marvellous sunny, Mediterranean flavors that taste

especially good on summer days, and a selection of them would be

perfect as part of a buffet for a party. Don't forget that you can use

the grill to broil ingredients such as tomatoes, bell peppers, eggplant

and radicchio – it will give them an intense, smoky flavor that will

pervade the whole salad.

APPLE COLESLAW

. . .

There are many variations of this traditional salad; this recipe combines the sweet flavors of apple and carrot with a hint of celery. Prepare the salad in advance and chill until needed.

INGREDIENTS

1 pound white cabbage
1 medium onion
2 apples, peeled and cored
6 ounces carrots, peeled
⅔ cup mayonnaise
1 teaspoon celery salt
freshly ground black pepper

SERVES 4

1 Remove the outer leaves from the cabbage and, using a heavy knife, cut it into 2-inch wedges. Remove and discard the stem sections.

2 Feed the cabbage wedges and the onion through the slicing blade of a food processor. Change to a grating blade and grate the apples and carrots. If you do not have a food processor, use a vegetable slicer and a hand grater.

3 Combine the salad ingredients in a large mixing bowl. Fold in the mayonnaise and season with celery salt and freshly ground black pepper. Garnish with apple slices and parsley.

Cook's Tip

This recipe can be adapted easily to suit different tastes. Add ½ cup chopped walnuts or raisins for added texture, or, for a richer, more substantial coleslaw, add ½ cup grated Cheddar cheese.

TOMATO AND FETA CHEESE SALAD

• • •

Sweet sun-ripened tomatoes are rarely more delicious than when mixed with feta cheese and olive oil. This salad can be served with any grilled meats, fish or vegetables.

INGREDIENTS

2 pounds tomatoes
7 ounces feta cheese
½ cup olive oil
12 black olives
4 sprigs fresh basil
freshly ground black pepper

SERVES 4

3 Crumble the feta cheese over the tomatoes, sprinkle with olive oil, then sprinkle with olives and fresh basil. Season with freshly ground black pepper and serve at room temperature.

1 Remove the tough cores from the tomatoes with a small kitchen knife.

2 Slice the tomatoes thickly on a chopping board and arrange the slices in a wide, shallow dish.

Cook's Tip

Feta cheese has a strong flavor and can be very salty. For an authentic flavor and texture, look for Greek, Cypriot or Turkish feta.

CURLY ENDIVE SALAD WITH BACON

• • •

When they are in season, young dandelion leaves could be included in this hearty French salad.
If you wish, sprinkle the salad with chopped hard-boiled egg.

2 Heat 1 tablespoon oil in a pan over medium heat and add the bacon. Fry until browned. Remove the bacon and drain on paper towels.

3 Add another 2 tablespoons oil to the pan and fry the bread cubes over medium heat, turning frequently, until browned. Remove the bread cubes with a slotted spoon and drain on paper towels. Discard any remaining fat.

INGREDIENTS

6 cups curly endive or escarole
leaves
5–6 tablespoons extra virgin
olive oil
6-ounce piece of smoked bacon,
diced
thick slice of white bread, cubed
1 small garlic clove, finely chopped
1 tablespoon red wine vinegar
2 teaspoons Dijon mustard
salt and freshly ground black
pepper

SERVES 4

1 Tear the lettuce leaves into bite-size pieces and put them in a large salad bowl. Set the bowl aside.

4 Stir the garlic, vinegar and mustard into the pan with the remaining oil and warm through. Season to taste. Pour the dressing over the salad and sprinkle with the fried bacon and croutons.

POTATO SALAD WITH SAUSAGE

The addition of garlic sausage makes this a substantial salad to serve as part of a buffet, but if it is to accompany grilled meat or fish you can make it with potatoes alone.

INGREDIENTS

1 pound small waxy potatoes
2–3 tablespoons dry white wine
2 shallots, finely chopped
1 tablespoon chopped fresh parsley
1 tablespoon chopped fresh tarragon
6 ounces French garlic sausage
fresh parsley, to garnish
salt and freshly ground black pepper

FOR THE VINAIGRETTE
2 teaspoons Dijon mustard
1 tablespoon tarragon vinegar or white wine vinegar
5 tablespoons extra virgin olive oil

SERVES 4

1 Cook the potatoes in boiling salted water for 10–15 minutes, until tender. Drain them, and refresh under cold running water. Cut them into ¼-inch slices, place them in a large bowl and sprinkle with the white wine and the chopped shallots.

2 To make the vinaigrette, mix the Dijon mustard and vinegar in a small bowl, then whisk in the olive oil, 1 tablespoon at a time. Season well with salt and freshly ground black and pour over the potatoes.

3 Add the chopped fresh parsley and tarragon to the potatoes in the bowl and toss until well mixed.

4 Slice the garlic sausage thinly and toss with the potatoes. Season with salt and pepper to taste and serve at room temperature, garnished with parsley.

GREEN BEAN SALAD WITH EGG TOPPING

• • •

When green beans are fresh and plentiful, serve them lightly cooked as a salad topped with
butter-fried bread crumbs, egg and fresh parsley.

INGREDIENTS

1½ pounds green beans,
trimmed
2 tablespoons extra virgin olive oil
2 tablespoons butter
1 cup fresh white bread crumbs
4 tablespoons chopped fresh
parsley
1 egg, hard-boiled and shelled
salt

SERVES 4

1 Bring a large pan of salted water
to a boil. Add the beans and cook for
6 minutes. Drain well, toss the beans
in olive oil and allow to cool.

2 Heat the butter in a large frying
pan, add the bread crumbs and fry
until golden. Remove the pan from the
heat, add the chopped fresh parsley,
then grate in the hard-boiled egg.

3 Place the beans in a shallow
serving dish and spoon on the bread
crumb topping. If preparing the salad
in advance and chilling it until needed,
allow it to come to room temperature
before serving.

TABBOULEH

. . .

*This classic Lebanese salad has become very popular everywhere. It makes an ideal substitute
for a rice dish and is especially good with grilled lamb.*

INGREDIENTS

1 cup fine bulgur
juice of 1 lemon
3 tablespoons olive oil
3/4 cup chopped fresh parsley
3 tablespoons fresh mint, chopped
4–5 scallions, chopped
1 green bell pepper, sliced
*salt and freshly ground black
pepper*
*2 large tomatoes, diced, and black
olives, to garnish*

SERVES 4

1 Put the bulgur in a large bowl.
Add enough cold water to cover and let
it stand for at least 30 minutes and up
to 2 hours.

2 Drain and squeeze the bulgur
with your hands to remove excess
water. The bulgur will swell to double
its original size. Spread the bulgur
evenly on paper towels to allow to
dry completely.

3 Place the bulgur in a large bowl
and add the lemon juice, the olive oil
and a little salt and pepper. Allow to
stand for 1–2 hours if possible, in
order for the flavors to develop.

4 Add the chopped parsley, mint,
scallions and pepper to the bowl and
mix well. Garnish with diced tomatoes
and olives and serve. The tabbouleh
can be prepared in advance, covered
with plastic wrap and stored in the
refrigerator until needed.

PEPPERS WITH TOMATOES AND ANCHOVIES

This is a Sicilian-style salad full of warm Mediterranean flavors. The salad improves if it is made and dressed an hour or two before serving.

INGREDIENTS

1 red bell pepper
1 yellow bell pepper
4 ripe plum tomatoes, sliced
2 canned anchovies, drained and
chopped
4 sun-dried tomatoes in oil,
drained and sliced
1 tablespoon capers, drained
1 tablespoon pine nuts
1 garlic clove, very finely sliced

FOR THE DRESSING
5 tablespoons extra virgin olive oil
1 tablespoon balsamic vinegar
1 teaspoon lemon juice
chopped fresh mixed herbs
salt and freshly ground black
pepper

SERVES 4

1 Cut the peppers in half and remove the seeds and stalks. Cut into quarters and cook, skin side down, over a hot grill or under the broiler until the skin chars. Transfer to a bowl and let cool. Peel the peppers and cut into strips.

2 Arrange the peppers and fresh tomatoes on a serving dish. Sprinkle the anchovies, sun-dried tomatoes, capers, pine nuts and garlic on top.

3 To make the dressing, mix together the olive oil, vinegar, lemon juice and chopped fresh herbs and season with plenty of salt and pepper. Pour the dressing over the salad before serving.

SWEET AND SOUR ONION SALAD

This recipe for tangy glazed onions in the Provençal style makes an unusual and flavorful accompaniment to grilled steaks.

INGREDIENTS

1 pound baby onions, peeled
¼ cup wine vinegar
3 tablespoons olive oil
3 tablespoons sugar
3 tablespoons tomato paste
1 bay leaf
2 parsley sprigs
½ cup raisins
salt and freshly ground black
pepper

SERVES 6

1 Put all the ingredients in a pan with 1¼ cups water. Bring to a boil and simmer gently, uncovered, for 45 minutes, or until the onions are tender and the liquid has evaporated.

2 Remove the bay leaf and parsley from the pan and check the seasoning. Transfer the contents of the pan to a large serving dish. Serve the salad at room temperature.

WARM FAVA BEAN AND FETA SALAD

This recipe is loosely based on a typical medley of fresh-tasting salad ingredients—
fava beans, tomatoes and feta cheese. It's lovely either warm or cold.

INGREDIENTS

2 pounds fresh fava beans, or
12 ounces frozen fava beans
4 tablespoons olive oil
6 ounces plum tomatoes, halved,
or quartered if large
4 garlic cloves, crushed
4 ounces firm feta cheese, cut into
chunks
3 tablespoons chopped fresh dill,
plus extra to garnish
12 black olives
salt and freshly ground black
pepper

SERVES 4–6

1 Shell the fava beans, then cook them in boiling, salted water until they are just tender. Drain and set aside.

2 Meanwhile, heat the olive oil in a heavy frying pan and add the tomatoes and garlic. Cook until the tomatoes are beginning to color.

3 Add the feta to the frying pan and toss the ingredients together for 1 minute. Mix with the drained beans, dill, olives and salt and pepper. Serve garnished with the chopped fresh dill.

GRILLED HALOUMI AND GRAPE SALAD

In the eastern Mediterranean, haloumi cheese is often served grilled or fried for breakfast or supper. In this recipe it's tossed with sweet, juicy grapes, which complement its distinctive flavor.

INGREDIENTS

5 ounces mixed green salad leaves
3 ounces seedless green grapes
3 ounces seedless black grapes
9 ounces haloumi cheese
2 tablespoons olive oil
fresh young thyme leaves or dill, to
garnish

FOR THE DRESSING
4 tablespoons olive oil
1 tablespoon lemon juice
1/2 teaspoon sugar
1 tablespoon chopped fresh thyme
or dill
salt and freshly ground black
pepper

SERVES 4

1 To make the dressing, mix the olive oil, lemon juice and sugar together in a bowl. Season with plenty of salt and black pepper. Stir in the chopped fresh thyme or dill and set aside.

2 Toss together the mixed green salad leaves and the green and black grapes, then transfer to a large serving plate or salad bowl.

3 Slice the haloumi cheese. Brush the slices with olive oil and cook briefly over a medium grill, or pan-fry on the stove, until golden, turning once.

4 Arrange the cooked cheese on top of the salad. Pour the dressing over it and garnish with thyme or dill leaves.

CHORIZO IN OLIVE OIL

• • •

Spanish chorizo sausage has a deliciously pungent taste. Frying chorizo with onions and olive oil
is one of the best ways of using it; you can also cook it on the grill, brushed with olive oil.

INGREDIENTS

5 tablespoons extra virgin olive oil
12 ounces chorizo sausage, sliced
1 large onion, thinly sliced
flat leaf parsley, roughly chopped,
to garnish

SERVES 4

1 Heat the olive oil in a frying pan
and fry the chorizo over high heat until
beginning to color. Remove from the
pan with a slotted spoon.

2 Add the onion slices to the pan
and fry until golden. Return the
sausage slices to the pan for about
1 minute to heat through.

3 Pour the mixture into a shallow
serving dish and sprinkle with the
chopped flat leaf parsley. Serve
the chorizo on its own or as a side
dish, with warm crusty bread.

Variation

Chorizo is usually available
in large supermarkets and
delicatessens, but any other
similar spicy sausage can be
used as a substitute.

FAVA BEAN, MUSHROOM AND CHORIZO SALAD

*This salad can be served as a first course or as part of a buffet menu. Prepare it a day
in advance and store it in the refrigerator until needed.*

INGREDIENTS

8 ounces shelled fava beans
6 ounces chorizo sausage
4 tablespoons extra virgin olive oil
8 ounces crimini mushrooms,
sliced
handful of fresh chives
salt and freshly ground black
pepper

SERVES 4

1 Cook the beans in a large saucepan
of boiling, salted water until just
tender. Drain and refresh under cold
running water. If the beans are large,
peel away the tough outer skins.

2 Remove the skin from the chorizo
and cut it into small chunks. Heat the
oil in a frying pan, add the chorizo and
cook for 2 minutes. Empty into a bowl
with the mushrooms, mix well and set
aside to cool.

3 Chop half the chives and stir the
beans and chopped chives into the
mushroom mixture. Season to taste.
Serve the salad at room temperature,
garnished with the remaining chives.

BABY EGGPLANTS WITH RAISINS AND PINE NUTS

∘ ∘ ∘

This is a recipe with an Italian influence, in a style that would have been familiar in Renaissance times. If possible, make it a day in advance, to allow the sweet and sour flavors to develop.

INGREDIENTS

12 baby eggplants, halved
1 cup extra virgin olive oil
juice of 1 lemon
2 tablespoons balsamic vinegar
3 cloves
$^1/_3$ cup pine nuts
2 tablespoons raisins
1 tablespoon sugar
1 bay leaf
large pinch of crushed red pepper
salt and freshly ground black pepper

SERVES 4

1 Brush the eggplants with olive oil and cook over a hot grill for about 10 minutes, until charred, turning once.

2 To make the dressing, combine the remaining olive oil with the lemon juice, vinegar, cloves, pine nuts, raisins, sugar and bay leaf. Add the red pepper, salt and pepper and mix well.

3 Place the hot eggplants in an earthenware or glass bowl and pour the dressing over them. Let cool, turning the eggplants once or twice. Serve the salad at room temperature.

SQUASH A LA GRECQUE

This salad makes a wonderful side dish for almost any barbecue meal. Cook the baby squash until they are perfectly tender, so that they can fully absorb the delicious flavors of the dressing.

INGREDIENTS

6 ounces pattypan squash
1 cup white wine
juice of 2 lemons
sprig of fresh thyme
1 bay leaf
handful of fresh chervil, roughly chopped
1/4 teaspoon coriander seeds, crushed
5 tablespoons olive oil
salt and freshly ground black pepper

SERVES 4

3 Reduce the liquid by boiling rapidly for 10 minutes. Strain it and pour it over the squash. Let sit until cool for the flavors to be absorbed.

1 Blanch the pattypan squash in boiling water for 3 minutes, drain, then refresh under cold running water.

2 Place the remaining ingredients in a pan, add 2/3 cup water and bring to a simmer. Add the squash and cook for 10 minutes, then remove it.

SALSAS, DIPS AND MARINADES

❦

The powerful flavors of grilled meat and fish call for spicy, lively

accompaniments. Chunky salsas are ideal, with their intriguing

combination of cool, crisp ingredients and fiery flavors. Tangy barbecue

sauce is a more traditional alternative that children adore. For a subtler

effect, melt a pat of butter flavored with herbs, garlic or anchovies over

a plainly grilled steak or fish. This chapter also includes some appetizing

dips to go with potato chips, bread sticks and crudités, and a selection

of delicious marinades suitable for a wide variety of meat and fish.

CHUNKY CHERRY TOMATO SALSA

· · ·

Succulent cherry tomatoes and refreshing cucumber form the base of this delicious dill-seasoned salsa. Prepare up to a day in advance and store in the refrigerator until needed.

INGREDIENTS

1 cucumber
1 teaspoon sea salt
1¼ pound cherry tomatoes
grated rind and juice of 1 lemon
3 tablespoons chili oil
½ teaspoon crushed red pepper
2 tablespoons chopped fresh dill
1 garlic clove, finely chopped
salt and freshly ground black
pepper

SERVES 4

1 Trim the ends off the cucumber and cut it into 1-inch lengths, then cut each piece lengthwise into thin slices. Place in a colander and sprinkle with sea salt. Let sit for 5 minutes.

2 Rinse the cucumber slices under cold water and dry with paper towels.

3 Quarter the cherry tomatoes and place in a bowl with the cucumber.

4 Whisk together the lemon rind and juice, chili oil, crushed red pepper, dill and garlic. Season, then pour over the tomato and cucumber and toss well. Marinate for 2 hours before serving.

Cook's Tip

Try flavoring the salsa with other herbs: tarragon, cilantro or mint.

SALSA VERDE

There are many versions of this classic green salsa. Try this one drizzled over grilled squid, or with baked potatoes.

INGREDIENTS

2–4 fresh green chilies, halved
8 scallions
2 garlic cloves
2 ounces salted capers
sprig of fresh tarragon
bunch of fresh parsley
grated rind and juice of 1 lime
juice of 1 lemon
6 tablespoons olive oil
1 tablespoon green Tabasco sauce, to taste
freshly ground black pepper

SERVES 4

1 Seed the chilies and trim the scallions. Halve the garlic cloves. Place in a food processor and pulse briefly.

2 Use your fingers to rub the excess salt off the capers. Add them, with the tarragon and parsley, to the food processor and pulse again until the ingredients are finely chopped.

3 Transfer the mixture to a large bowl. Mix in the lime rind and juice, lemon juice and olive oil, stirring lightly so that the citrus juice and oil do not emulsify.

4 Add green Tabasco sauce, a little at a time, and black pepper to taste. Chill the salsa in the refrigerator until ready to serve, but do not prepare it more than 8 hours in advance.

FIERY CITRUS SALSA
∘ ∘ ∘

This unusual salsa makes a fantastic marinade for shellfish; it's also
delicious drizzled over grilled meat.

INGREDIENTS

1 orange
1 green apple
2 fresh red chilies
1 garlic clove
8 fresh mint leaves
juice of 1 lemon
salt and freshly ground black
pepper

SERVES 4

1 Using a sharp knife, remove the peel and pith from the orange and, working over a bowl to catch the juices, cut out the segments. Squeeze any remaining juice into the bowl.

2 Use a sharp kitchen knife to peel the apple and slice it into wedges. Remove and discard the apple core.

3 Halve the chilies and remove the seeds, then place them in a blender or food processor with the orange segments and juice, apple wedges, garlic and mint.

4 Process until smooth. With the motor running, slowly pour in the lemon juice. Season to taste with salt and freshly ground black pepper and serve immediately.

FRESH CORN SALSA

• • •

Serve this succulent salsa with grilled ham or pork, or with smoked meats. The charbroiled fresh corn makes the salsa particularly flavorful.

INGREDIENTS

2 ears of fresh corn
2 tablespoons melted butter
4 tomatoes
6 scallions, finely chopped
1 garlic clove, finely chopped
2 tablespoons lemon juice
2 tablespoons olive oil
red Tabasco sauce, to taste
salt and freshly ground black
pepper

SERVES 4

3 Skewer the tomatoes and hold them over the grill or broil them for about 2 minutes, turning, until the skin splits and wrinkles. Slip off the skins and dice the flesh. Add to the corn with the scallions and chopped garlic.

4 Stir the lemon juice and olive oil together, adding Tabasco, salt and black pepper to taste. Pour mixture over the salsa, stir well, cover and set aside to marinate at room temperature for 1–2 hours before serving.

1 Remove the husks and silks from the corn. Brush with the melted butter and gently grill or broil for about 20 minutes, turning occasionally, until tender and charred.

2 To remove the kernels, stand each ear upright on a chopping board and use a large, heavy knife to slice down its length. Put the kernels in a mixing bowl.

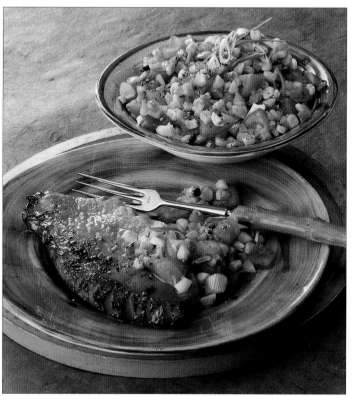

BARBECUE SAUCE

• • •

Brush this sauce liberally over chicken pieces, chops or kebabs before cooking on the grill, or
serve as a hot or cold accompaniment to hot dogs and hamburgers.

INGREDIENTS

2 tablespoons vegetable oil
1 large onion, chopped
2 garlic cloves, crushed
14-ounce can tomatoes
2 tablespoons Worcestershire sauce
1 tablespoon white wine vinegar
3 tablespoons honey
1 teaspoon mustard powder
½ teaspoon chili seasoning or mild
chili powder
salt and freshly ground black
pepper

SERVES **4**

3 Pour into a food processor or blender and process until smooth.

4 Press through a sieve if you like. Adjust the seasoning to taste.

1 Heat the vegetable oil in a large saucepan and fry the onions and garlic until soft and golden.

2 Stir in the remaining ingredients and simmer, uncovered, for 15–20 minutes, stirring occasionally. Remove the saucepan from the heat and allow to cool slightly.

GUACAMOLE

. . .

Nachos or tortilla chips are the classic accompaniments for this classic Mexican dip, but it also tastes great served on the side with burgers or kebabs.

INGREDIENTS

2 ripe avocados
2 red chilies, seeded
1 garlic clove
1 shallot
2 tablespoons olive oil, plus
extra to serve
juice of 1 lemon
salt
fresh flat leaf parsley, to garnish

SERVES 4

1 Halve the avocados, flick out the pits using the point of a sharp knife, and use a teaspoon to scoop the flesh into a large bowl.

2 Mash the flesh well, using a potato masher or a large fork, so that the avocado is a fairly smooth consistency.

3 Finely chop the chilies, garlic clove and shallot, then stir into the mashed avocado with the olive oil and lemon juice. Add salt to taste and mix well.

4 Spoon the mixture into a serving bowl. Drizzle on a little more olive oil and sprinkle with flat leaf parsley leaves. Guacamole will not keep for very long but can be prepared up to 8 hours in advance and stored in the refrigerator, sprinkled with lemon juice and covered with plastic wrap.

CARAMELIZED ONION RELISH
∘ ∘ ∘

Slow, gentle cooking reduces the onions to a soft, sweet relish, which would make a tasty addition to many barbecue menus.

2 Heat the butter and oil together in a large saucepan. Add the onions and sugar and cook very gently for 30 minutes over low heat, stirring occasionally, until reduced to a soft rich brown caramelized mixture.

3 Roughly chop the capers and stir them into the caramelized onions. Allow to cool completely.

4 Stir in the chopped fresh parsley and add salt and pepper to taste. Cover with plastic wrap and chill in the refrigerator until ready to serve.

INGREDIENTS

3 large onions
4 tablespoons butter
2 tablespoons olive oil
2 tablespoons light brown sugar
2 tablespoons capers
2 tablespoons chopped fresh parsley
salt and freshly ground black pepper

SERVES 4

1 Peel the onions and halve them vertically through the core, using a sharp knife. Slice them thinly.

PARSLEY BUTTER

° ° °

This butter, or one of the variations below, makes a subtle accompaniment to
grilled food, particularly fish with a delicate flavor.

INGREDIENTS

8 tablespoons softened butter
2 tablespoons finely chopped parsley
½ teaspoon lemon juice
cayenne pepper
salt and freshly ground black pepper

SERVES 4

1 Beat the butter until creamy, then beat in the parsley, lemon juice and cayenne pepper, and season lightly.

2 Spread the butter ¼ inch thick onto a piece of foil, chill, then cut into shapes with a knife or cookie cutter.

3 Alternatively, form the butter into a roll, wrap in plastic wrap or foil and chill. Cut off slices as required.

Variations

LEMON OR LIME BUTTER
Add 1 tablespoon finely grated
lemon or lime rind and
1 tablespoon juice to the butter.

HERB BUTTER
Replace the parsley with
2 tablespoons chopped mint,
chives or tarragon.

GARLIC BUTTER
Add 2 crushed garlic cloves
to the butter with 1–2 tablespoons
chopped parsley.

ANCHOVY BUTTER
Add 6 anchovy fillets, drained of
oil and mashed with a fork, to the
butter. Season with pepper only.

MUSTARD BUTTER
Add 2 teaspoons English mustard
and 2 tablespoons chopped chives
to the butter.

These butters will keep in
the refrigerator for several days,
and will also freeze well, wrapped
in plastic wrap or foil to prevent
any loss of flavor.

CREAMY EGGPLANT DIP

Spread this velvet-textured dip thickly on slices of French bread toasted on the grill, then top with slivers of sun-dried tomato to make wonderful Italian-style crostini.

INGREDIENTS

1 large eggplant
2 tablespoons olive oil
1 small onion, finely chopped
2 garlic cloves, finely chopped
4 tablespoons chopped fresh parsley
5 tablespoons crème fraîche
red Tabasco sauce, to taste
juice of 1 lemon, to taste
salt and freshly ground black pepper

SERVES 4

3 Peel the eggplant and mash the flesh with a large fork or potato masher to make a pulpy purée.

4 Stir in the onion and garlic, parsley and crème fraîche. Add Tabasco, lemon juice, and salt and pepper. Serve warm.

1 Cook the whole eggplant on a medium grill or broil for about 20 minutes, turning occasionally, until the skin is blackened and the eggplant soft. Cover the eggplant with a clean dish towel and set aside to cool for about 5 minutes.

2 Heat the oil in a frying pan and cook the chopped onion and garlic for 5 minutes, until soft but not browned.

FAT-FREE SAFFRON DIP

. . .

Serve this mild dip with fresh vegetable crudités—it is particularly good with florets of cauliflower, asparagus tips and baby carrots and corn.

INGREDIENTS

1 tablespoon boiling water
small pinch saffron strands
scant 1 cup fat-free fromage frais
10 fresh chives
10 fresh basil leaves
salt and freshly ground black
pepper

SERVES 4

1 Pour the boiling water into a bowl and add the saffron strands. Allow to infuse for 3 minutes.

2 Beat the fromage frais in a large bowl until smooth. Stir in the infused saffron liquid with a wooden spoon.

Cook's Tip

If you don't have any saffron, add a squeeze of lemon or lime juice.

3 Snip the chives into the dip. Tear the basil leaves into small pieces and stir them in. Mix thoroughly.

4 Add salt and freshly ground black pepper to taste. Serve the dip with fresh vegetable crudités, if desired.

SPICY YOGURT MARINADE

• • •

*Use this marinade for chicken, lamb or pork, and marinate the meat, covered and chilled,
for 24 to 36 hours to develop a mellow spicy flavor.*

INGREDIENTS

1 teaspoon coriander seeds
2 teaspoons cumin seeds
6 cloves
2 bay leaves
1 onion, quartered
2 garlic cloves
2-inch piece fresh ginger, roughly
chopped
1/2 teaspoon chili powder
1 teaspoon ground turmeric
2/3 cup plain yogurt
juice of 1 lemon

SERVES 6

1 Spread the coriander and cumin seeds, cloves and bay leaves over the bottom of a large frying pan and dry-fry over moderate heat until the bay leaves are crisp.

3 Finely chop the onion, garlic and ginger in a blender or food processor. Add the ground spices, chili powder, turmeric, yogurt and lemon juice.

4 If you are marinating chicken parts or large pieces of meat, make several deep slashes to allow the flavors to penetrate. Arrange the pieces in a single layer and pour the marinade over them. Cover and place in the refrigerator to marinate for at least 24 hours.

Cook's Tip

Garnish the finished dish with fresh cilantro leaves and slices of lemon or lime.

2 Allow the spices to cool, then grind coarsely with a mortar and pestle.

ORANGE AND GREEN PEPPERCORN MARINADE

* * *

This is an excellent light marinade for delicately flavored whole fish such as sea trout, bass or bream. The beauty of the fish is perfectly set off by the softly colored marinade.

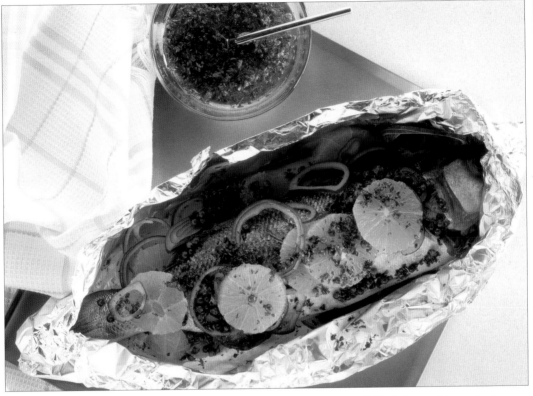

3 Mix the remaining marinade ingredients and pour over the fish. Cover and let marinate for 4 hours, occasionally spooning the marinade over the fish.

4 Fold the foil loosely over the fish and seal the edges securely. Bake on a medium grill for 15 minutes for 1 pound, plus 15 minutes more.

INGREDIENTS

1 red onion
2 small oranges
6 tablespoons light olive oil
2 tablespoons cider vinegar
2 tablespoons green peppercorns in brine, drained
2 tablespoons chopped fresh parsley
salt and sugar

FOR 1 MEDIUM-SIZE FISH

1 With a sharp knife, slash the fish 3 or 4 times on each side.

2 Cut a piece of foil big enough to wrap the fish and use to line a large dish. Peel and slice the onion and oranges. Lay half the slices on the foil, place the fish on top and cover with the remaining onion and orange.

203

GINGER AND LIME MARINADE

· · ·

This fragrant marinade will guarantee a mouthwatering aroma from the grill. Shown here on shrimp and monkfish kebabs, it is just as delicious with chicken or pork.

INGREDIENTS

3 limes
1 tablespoon green cardamom pods
1 onion, finely chopped
1-inch piece fresh ginger, grated
1 large garlic clove, crushed
3 tablespoons olive oil

SERVES 4–6

3 Mix all the marinade ingredients together and pour over the meat or fish. Stir gently, cover and set aside in a cool place to marinate for 2–3 hours.

4 Drain the meat or fish when you are ready to cook it on the grill. Baste the meat occasionally with the marinade while cooking.

1 Finely grate the rind from one lime and squeeze the juice from all of them.

2 Split the cardamom pods and remove the seeds. Crush with a mortar and pestle or the back of a heavy-bladed knife.

SUMMER HERB MARINADE

· o o

Make the best use of summer herbs in this marinade. Try any combination of herbs, depending on what you have on hand, and use with veal, chicken, pork, lamb or salmon.

INGREDIENTS

large handful of fresh herb sprigs, e.g. chervil, thyme, parsley, sage, chives, rosemary, oregano
6 tablespoons olive oil
3 tablespoons tarragon vinegar
1 garlic clove, crushed
2 scallions, chopped
salt and freshly ground black pepper

SERVES 4

3 Place the meat or fish in a bowl and pour the marinade over it. Cover and set aside to marinate in a cool place for 4–6 hours.

4 Drain the meat or fish when you are ready to cook it on the grill. Use the marinade to baste the meat occasionally while cooking.

1 Discard any coarse stalks or damaged leaves from the herbs, then chop them very finely.

2 Add the chopped herbs to the remaining marinade ingredients in a large bowl. Stir to mix thoroughly.

DESSERTS

━━◆━━

At the end of a barbecue it's a lovely idea to use the lingering fire

to make a delicious fruity dessert. You can cook fruit to melting

tenderness by wrapping it in foil, including sugar, spices and a sprinkling

of liqueur in the parcel. To broil fruit, cut it into chunks and spear it on

skewers, or just lay large slices on the grill rack. Sprinkle it with sugar

to caramelize in the heat. The aroma is intoxicating: even those who

thought they couldn't eat another bite will be beguiled by it. Accompany

grilled fruit with a buttery, spicy sauce, crisp toasted brioche or freshly

made griddle cakes – and perhaps a scoop of whipped cream or

ice cream – to make a perfect end to the meal.

PINEAPPLE WEDGES WITH RUM BUTTER GLAZE

∘ ∘ ∘

Fresh pineapple is even more full of flavor when grilled, and this spiced rum glaze makes it into a very special dessert.

INGREDIENTS

1 medium pineapple
2 tablespoons dark brown sugar
1 teaspoon ground ginger
4 tablespoons melted butter
2 tablespoons dark rum

SERVES 4

1 With a large, sharp knife, cut the pineapple lengthwise into 4 wedges. Cut out and discard the central core.

2 Cut between the flesh and skin, to release the skin, but leave the flesh in place. Slice the flesh across and lengthwise to make thick chunks.

3 Soak 4 bamboo skewers in water for 15 minutes to prevent them from scorching on the grill. Push a skewer through each wedge, into the stalk, to hold the chunks in place.

4 Mix together the sugar, ginger, butter and rum and brush over the pineapple. Cook the wedges on the grill for 4 minutes; pour the remaining glaze over the top and serve.

Cook's Tip

For an easier version, simply remove the skin and then cut the whole pineapple into thick slices and cook as directed.

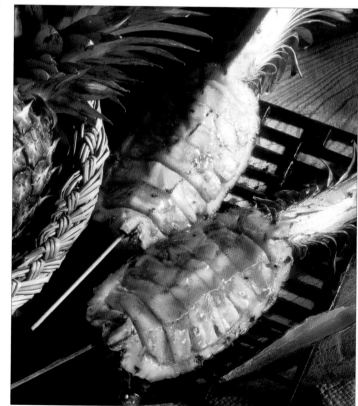

BAKED BANANAS WITH SPICY VANILLA FILLING

° ° °

Bananas are ideal for barbecue cooking, as they bake in their skins and need no preparation at all. This flavored butter adds richness; children may prefer melted chocolate, jam or honey.

INGREDIENTS

4 bananas
6 green cardamom pods
1 vanilla bean
finely grated rind of 1 small orange
2 tablespoons brandy or orange juice
4 tablespoons light brown sugar
3 tablespoons butter
crème fraîche or strained plain
yogurt, to serve

SERVES 4

1 Place the bananas, in their skins, on a hot grill and cook for 6–8 minutes, turning occasionally, until they are turning brownish black.

2 Meanwhile, split the cardamom pods and remove the seeds. Crush lightly with a mortar and pestle.

3 Split the vanilla bean lengthwise and scrape out the tiny seeds. Mix with the cardamom seeds, orange rind, brandy or juice, brown sugar and butter into a thick paste.

4 Using a sharp knife, slit the skin of each banana, then open out the skin and spoon in a little of the paste. Serve with a spoonful of crème fraîche or yogurt, if desired.

ORANGES IN MAPLE AND COINTREAU SYRUP

• • •

*This is one of the most delicious ways to eat an orange, and a luxurious way to round off
a barbecue. For a children's or alcohol-free version, omit the liqueur.*

INGREDIENTS

*4 teaspoons butter, plus extra,
melted, for brushing
4 medium oranges
2 tablespoons maple syrup
2 tablespoons Cointreau or Grand
Marnier liqueur
crème fraîche or fromage frais,
to serve*

SERVES 4

2 Remove some shreds of orange rind, to decorate. Blanch these, dry them and set them aside. Peel the oranges, removing all the white pith and catching the juice in a bowl.

4 Tuck the foil up securely around the oranges so that they keep their shape, leaving the foil open at the top.

1 Cut 4 double-thickness squares of aluminum foil, large enough to wrap each of the oranges. Brush the center of each square of foil with plenty of melted butter.

3 Slice the oranges crosswise into thick slices. Reassemble them and place each orange on a square of baking foil.

5 Mix together the reserved orange juice, maple syrup and liqueur and spoon the mixture over the oranges.

6 Add a pat of butter to each parcel and close the foil at the top to seal in the juices. Place the parcels on a hot grill for 10–12 minutes, until hot. Serve with crème fraîche or fromage frais, topped with the reserved shreds of orange rind.

NECTARINES WITH MARZIPAN AND MASCARPONE

A luscious dessert that no one can resist—dieters may prefer to use low-fat cream cheese or plain yogurt instead of mascarpone.

INGREDIENTS

4 firm, ripe nectarines or peaches
3 ounces marzipan
5 tablespoons mascarpone cheese
3 macaroons, crushed

SERVES 4

1 Cut the nectarines or peaches in half and remove the pits.

2 Divide the marzipan into 8 pieces, roll into balls, using your fingers, and press one piece of marzipan into the pit cavity of each nectarine half.

Cook's Tip

Either nectarines or peaches can be used for this recipe. If the pit does not pull out easily when you halve the fruit, use a small, sharp knife to cut around it.

3 Spoon the mascarpone cheese on top of the fruit halves. Sprinkle the crushed macaroons over the mascarpone.

4 Place the fruit halves on a hot grill for 3–5 minutes, until they are hot and the mascarpone starts to melt. Serve immediately.

GRILLED STRAWBERRY CROISSANTS

° ° °

The combination of crisp grilled croissants, ricotta cheese and sweet strawberry
preserves makes for a deliciously simple, sinful dessert.

INGREDIENTS

4 croissants
½ cup ricotta cheese
½ cup strawberry preserves
or jam

SERVES 4

3 Top the ricotta with a generous spoonful of strawberry preserves and replace the top half of the croissant.

4 Place the filled croissants on a hot grill and cook for 2–3 minutes, turning once. Serve immediately.

1 On a chopping board, split the croissants in half and open them out.

2 Spread the bottom half of each croissant with a generous layer of the ricotta cheese.

Cook's Tip

As an alternative to croissants, try scones, brioches or muffins, toasted on the grill.

GRIDDLE CAKES WITH MULLED PLUMS

• • •

These delectably light little pancakes are fun to make on the grill. They are served with a rich, spicy plum sauce.

INGREDIENTS

1¼ pounds red plums
6 tablespoons light brown sugar
1 cinnamon stick
2 whole cloves
1 piece star anise
6 tablespoons apple juice
cream or strained plain yogurt,
to serve

FOR THE GRIDDLE CAKES
½ cup all-purpose flour
2 teaspoons baking powder
pinch of salt
½ cup fine cornmeal
2 tablespoons light brown sugar
1 egg, beaten
1¼ cups milk
2 tablespoons corn oil

SERVES 6

2 Bring to a boil, then reduce the heat, cover the pan and simmer gently for 8–10 minutes, stirring occasionally, until the plums are soft. Remove the spices and keep the plums warm on the side of the grill.

5 Heat a griddle or a heavy frying pan on a hot grill. Brush with the remaining oil, then drop tablespoons of batter onto it, allowing them to spread. Cook the griddle cakes for about a minute, until bubbles start to appear on the surface and the underside is golden brown.

3 For the griddle cakes, sift the flour, baking powder and salt into a large mixing bowl and stir in the cornmeal and brown sugar.

6 Turn the cakes over and cook the other side for a minute more, or until golden. Serve the cakes hot from the griddle with a spoonful of mulled plums and cream or yogurt.

1 Halve, pit and quarter the plums. Place them in a flameproof pan, with the sugar, spices and apple juice.

Cook's Tip

If you prefer, make the griddle cakes in advance, on the stove, and then simply heat them for a few seconds on the grill to serve with the plums.

4 Make a well in the center of the dry ingredients and add the egg, then beat in the milk. Beat thoroughly with a whisk or wooden spoon to form a smooth batter. Beat in half the oil.

FRUIT KEBABS WITH CHOCOLATE FONDUE

∘ ∘ ∘

Fondues are always lots of fun, and the delicious ingredients used here—fresh fruit, chocolate and marshmallow—will make this recipe a popular choice with children and adults alike.

2 Mix together the butter, lemon juice and ground cinnamon and brush the mixture generously over the fruit.

3 For the fondue, place the chocolate, cream and marshmallows in a small pan and heat gently, without boiling, stirring constantly until the mixture has melted and is smooth.

INGREDIENTS

2 bananas
2 kiwi fruit
12 strawberries
1 tablespoon melted butter
1 tablespoon lemon juice
1 teaspoon ground cinnamon

FOR THE FONDUE
8 ounces semisweet chocolate
1/2 cup light cream
8 marshmallows
1/2 teaspoon vanilla extract

SERVES 4

1 Peel the bananas and cut into thick chunks. Peel the kiwi fruit and quarter them. Thread the bananas, kiwi fruit and strawberries onto 4 wooden skewers. (Soak the skewers in water for 15 minutes beforehand to prevent them scorching on the grill.)

4 Cook the kebabs on a medium-hot grill, turning once, for 2–3 minutes, or until the fruit is golden. Stir the vanilla extract into the fondue. Empty the fondue into a small bowl and serve at once, with the fruit kebabs.

SPICED PEAR AND BLUEBERRY PARCELS

• • •

This fruity combination makes a delicious dessert for a hot summer evening.
You could substitute other berries for the blueberries if you prefer.

INGREDIENTS

4 firm, ripe pears
2 tablespoons lemon juice
1 tablespoon melted butter
1¼ cups blueberries
4 tablespoons light brown sugar
freshly ground black pepper

SERVES 4

3 Cut 4 squares of double-thickness aluminum foil, large enough to wrap the pears, and brush them with melted butter. Place two pear halves on each, cut sides up. Gather the foil up around them, to hold them level.

4 Mix the blueberries and sugar together and spoon them over the pears. Sprinkle with black pepper. Seal the edges of the foil over the pears and cook on a fairly hot grill for about 20–25 minutes.

1 Peel the pears thinly. Cut them in half lengthwise. Scoop out the core from each half, using a teaspoon and a sharp kitchen knife.

2 Brush the pears with lemon juice, to prevent them from discoloring.

Cook's Tip

To assemble in advance, line with a layer of waxed paper, as the acid in the lemon juice may react with the foil and taint the flavor.

FRESH FIGS WITH VANILLA CREAM

· · ·

The ripeness of the figs will determine their cooking time. This is an ideal recipe for a barbecue because it is prepared on the grill and left to stand until you are ready to eat.

INGREDIENTS

2 cups dry white wine

1/3 cup clear honey

1/4 cup sugar

1 small orange

8 whole cloves

1 pound fresh figs

1 cinnamon stick

sprigs of fresh mint, or bay leaves,
to decorate

FOR THE VANILLA CREAM

1 1/4 cups double cream

1 vanilla bean

1 teaspoon sugar

SERVES 6

1 Put the wine, honey and sugar in a heavy saucepan and heat gently on the grill or stovetop until the sugar dissolves.

2 Stud the orange with the cloves and add to the syrup with the figs and cinnamon. Cover and simmer very gently for 5–10 minutes, until the figs are tender. Transfer the contents of the pan to a serving dish and let cool.

3 Put 2/3 cup of the cream in a small saucepan with the vanilla bean. Bring almost to a boil, then allow to cool and infuse for 30 minutes. Remove the vanilla bean and mix the flavored cream with the remaining cream and sugar in a bowl. Whip lightly. Transfer to a serving dish.

4 Decorate the figs with mint or bay leaves and serve with the vanilla cream.

BAKED APPLES IN HONEY AND LEMON

Tender, fluffy baked apples with a classic flavoring of lemon and honey make a simple,
traditional dessert. Serve with custard or a spoonful of whipped cream, if you wish.

INGREDIENTS

4 medium cooking apples
1 tablespoon honey
grated rind and juice of 1 lemon
1 tablespoon butter, melted

SERVES 4

1 Remove the cores from the apples, leaving them whole. Cut four squares of double-thickness aluminum foil, to wrap the apples, and brush with butter.

2 With a cannelle or sharp knife, cut lines through the apple skin at regular intervals.

3 Mix together the honey, lemon rind, juice and butter in a small bowl.

4 Spoon the mixture into the apples and wrap in foil, sealing the edges securely. Cook on a hot grill for 20 minutes, until the apples are tender.

221

POACHED PEARS IN MAPLE AND YOGURT SAUCE

This elegant dessert is easier to make than it looks—poach the pears on the stove or grill when you cook the main course, and have the cooled syrup ready to add just before serving.

INGREDIENTS

6 firm pears
1 tablespoon lemon juice
1 cup sweet white wine
or cider
thinly pared rind of 1 lemon
1 cinnamon stick
2 tablespoons maple syrup
½ teaspoon arrowroot
⅔ cup strained plain yogurt

SERVES 6

1 Peel the pears, leaving them whole and with stalks. Brush with lemon juice to prevent them from discoloring. Use a potato peeler or small knife to scoop out the core from the bottom of each pear.

2 Place the pears in a wide, heavy pan and pour the wine over them, with enough cold water to almost cover the fruit. Add the lemon rind and cinnamon stick, and bring to a boil on the stove or, using a flameproof pan, on the grill. Reduce the heat, cover and simmer for 30 minutes, or until tender. Lift out the pears carefully.

3 Boil the remaining liquid, uncovered, until reduced to about ½ cup. Strain and add the maple syrup. Blend a little of the liquid with the arrowroot. Return to the pan and cook, stirring, until thick and clear. Allow to cool.

4 Slice each pear, leaving the slices attached at the stem end, and fan out on serving plates. Stir 2 tablespoons of the cooled syrup into the yogurt and spoon around the pears. Drizzle the pears with the remaining syrup and serve immediately.

CHOCOLATE MINT TRUFFLE FILO PARCELS

○ ○ ○

These exquisite little parcels are utterly irresistible: there will be no leftovers. The use of fresh mint in the recipe gives a wonderfully fresh flavor.

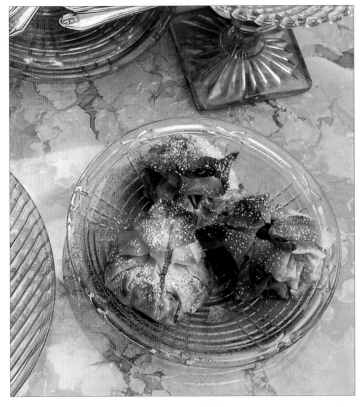

2 Cut the filo pastry sheets into 3-inch squares and cover with a damp cloth to prevent them from drying out.

3 Brush a square of filo with melted butter, lay on a second sheet, brush again and place a spoonful of filling in the middle of the top sheet. Bring in all four corners and twist to form a purse shape. Repeat to make 18 parcels.

4 Place the filo parcels on a griddle or baking sheet, well brushed with melted butter. Cook on a medium-hot grill for about 10 minutes, until the filo pastry is crisp. Let cool, then dust lightly with sifted confectioners' sugar and then with sifted cocoa powder.

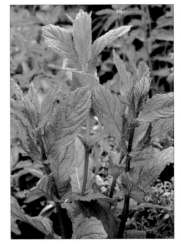

INGREDIENTS

1 tablespoon very finely chopped fresh mint
3/4 cup ground almonds
2 ounces semisweet chocolate, grated
1/2 cup crème fraîche
2 dessert apples, peeled and grated
9 large sheets filo pastry
5 1/3 tablespoons butter, melted
1 tablespoon confectioners' sugar
1 tablespoon cocoa powder

MAKES 18 PARCELS

1 Mix the chopped fresh mint, almonds, grated chocolate, crème fraîche and grated apple in a large mixing bowl. Set aside.

OUTDOOR ENTERTAINING

———◆———

Everything tastes better out of doors, and picnics – whether in the

garden, at the beach or in a grassy meadow – are a great pleasure both

to organize and to take part in, as long as the weather is kind. If you

have a portable grill you can take it along with you and make the food

twice as exciting, but take care that you light it in a safe place and clear

up carefully afterwards. Food for grilling can be transported in its

marinade, all ready to be popped over the heat. Pack interesting dips

into plastic boxes, and take pitas or prepared vegetables to go with

them. Homemade quiches and pies will also help to satisfy healthy

outdoor appetites. This section also offers inspirations for special

summer meals and garden parties at home, including some original

and delicious ideas for party drinks.

VEGETABLES WITH TAPENADE AND HERB AIOLI

○ ○ ○

A beautiful platter of summer vegetables served with one or two interesting sauces makes an enticing and informal appetizer that is perfect for picnics, since it can all be prepared in advance.

INGREDIENTS

2 red bell peppers, cut into wide strips
2 tablespoons olive oil
8 ounces new potatoes
4 ounces green beans
8 ounces baby carrots
8 ounces young asparagus
12 quail eggs
fresh herbs, to garnish
coarse salt, for sprinkling

FOR THE TAPENADE
1½ cups pitted black olives
2-ounce can anchovy fillets, drained
2 tablespoons capers
½ cup olive oil
finely grated rind of 1 lemon
1 tablespoon brandy (optional)
freshly ground black pepper

FOR THE HERB AIOLI
5 garlic cloves, crushed
2 egg yolks
1 teaspoon Dijon mustard
2 teaspoon white wine vinegar
1 cup light olive oil
3 tablespoons chopped mixed fresh herbs, such as chervil, parsley and tarragon
2 tablespoons chopped watercress
salt and freshly ground black pepper

SERVES 6

1 To make the tapenade, finely chop the olives, anchovies and capers and beat together with the oil, lemon rind and brandy, if using. (Alternatively, lightly process the ingredients in a blender or food processor.)

2 Season with pepper and blend in a little more oil if the mixture seems very dry. Transfer to a serving dish.

3 To make the aïoli, beat together the garlic, egg yolks, mustard and vinegar. Gradually blend in the olive oil, a drop at a time, whisking well until thick and smooth.

4 Stir in the mixed herbs and watercress. Season with salt and pepper to taste, adding a little more vinegar if necessary. Cover with plastic wrap and chill until ready to serve.

Cook's Tip
Any leftover tapenade is delicious tossed with pasta or spread on warm toast. If you are making this dish as part of a picnic, allow the vegetables to cool before packing in an airtight container. Pack the quail eggs in their original box.

5 Brush the peppers with oil and cook on a hot grill or under a hot broiler until just beginning to char.

6 Cook the potatoes in a large pan of boiling, salted water until tender. Add the beans and carrots and blanch for 1 minute. Add the asparagus and cook for another 30 seconds. Drain the vegetables. Cook the quail eggs in boiling water for 2 minutes.

7 Arrange all the vegetables, eggs and sauces on a serving platter. Garnish with fresh herbs and serve with coarse salt, for sprinkling.

TOMATO AND CHEESE TARTS

These crisp little tartlets look impressive but are actually very easy to make.
They are best eaten fresh from the oven.

INGREDIENTS
3 sheets filo pastry
1 egg white
6 ounces cream cheese
handful of fresh basil leaves
4 small tomatoes, sliced
salt and freshly ground black
pepper

MAKES 12

1 Preheat the oven to 400°F. Brush the sheets of filo pastry lightly with egg white and cut into 4-inch squares.

2 Layer the squares in twos, in 12 tartlet pans. Spoon the cream cheese into the pastry shells. Season with ground black pepper and top with fresh basil leaves.

3 Arrange the tomatoes on the tarts, season and bake for 10–12 minutes, until the pastry is golden. Serve warm.

Cook's Tip
Use halved cherry tomatoes for the tarts, if you prefer.

TANDOORI CHICKEN STICKS

These aromatic chicken pieces are traditionally baked in the special clay oven known as a tandoor. They are equally delicious served hot or cold, and make irresistible barbecue food.

INGREDIENTS

1 pound skinless, boneless chicken breasts

FOR THE CILANTRO YOGURT
1 cup plain yogurt
2 tablespoons whipping cream
1/2 cucumber, peeled, seeded and finely chopped
1–2 tablespoons fresh chopped cilantro or mint
salt and freshly ground black pepper

FOR THE MARINADE
3/4 cup plain yogurt
1 teaspoon garam masala or curry powder
1/4 teaspoon ground cumin
1/4 teaspoon ground coriander
1/4 teaspoon cayenne pepper (or to taste)
1 teaspoon tomato paste
1–2 garlic cloves, finely chopped
1-inch piece fresh ginger, finely chopped
grated zest and juice of 1/2 lemon
1–2 tablespoons fresh chopped cilantro or mint

MAKES ABOUT 25

2 To prepare the marinade, place all the ingredients in a food processor and process until smooth. Pour into a shallow dish.

3 Freeze the chicken breasts for 5 minutes to firm them, then slice in half horizontally. Cut the slices into 3/4-inch strips and add to the marinade. Toss to coat well. Cover with plastic wrap and chill for 6–8 hours or overnight.

4 Drain the chicken pieces and arrange on a rack, scrunching up the chicken slightly to make wavy shapes. Cook on a hot grill for 4–5 minutes, until brown and cooked through, turning once. Alternatively, arrange on a foil-lined baking sheet and cook under a hot broiler. Serve hot, threaded on toothpicks or short skewers, with the yogurt dip. For a picnic, allow to cool and pack into a box.

1 For the cilantro yogurt, combine all the ingredients in a bowl. Season, cover and chill until ready to serve.

HAM PIZZETTAS WITH MELTED BRIE AND MANGO

• • •

These little individual pizzas are topped with an unusual but very successful combination of smoked ham, Brie and juicy chunks of fresh mango.

INGREDIENTS

2 cups white bread flour
1/4-ounce envelope active
dry yeast
2/3 cup warm water
4 tablespoons olive oil

FOR THE TOPPING
1 ripe mango
5 ounces smoked ham, sliced
wafer-thin
5 ounces Brie cheese, diced
12 yellow cherry tomatoes,
halved
salt and freshly ground black
pepper

SERVES 6

1 In a large bowl, stir together the flour and yeast, with a pinch of salt. Make a well in the center and stir in the water and 3 tablespoons of the olive oil. Stir until thoroughly mixed.

Cook's Tip

It's important to flatten out the dough rounds quite thinly and to cook them fairly slowly, or they will not cook evenly. To save time, you could use an 11-ounce package of pizza-dough mix.

2 Turn the dough out onto a floured surface and knead it for about 5 minutes, or until smooth.

3 Return the dough to the bowl and cover it with a damp cloth or oiled plastic wrap. Set the dough aside in a warm place for about 30 minutes, or until it is doubled in size and springy to the touch.

4 Divide the dough into 6 pieces and roll each piece into a ball. Flatten out with your hand and use your knuckles to press each piece of dough into a round about 6 inches in diameter, with a raised lip around the edge.

5 Halve, pit and peel the mango and cut it into small dice. Arrange with the ham on top of the pizzettas. Top with cheese and tomatoes and sprinkle with salt and ground black pepper.

6 Drizzle the remaining oil over the pizzettas. Place them on a medium-hot grill and cook for 8 minutes, until golden brown and crisp underneath.

CHICKEN, MUSHROOM AND CILANTRO PIZZA

· · ·

Shiitake mushrooms add an earthy flavor to this colorful pizza, while fresh chili and chili-flavored olive oil give it a hint of spiciness. Cook the pizza on the grill or in the oven.

INGREDIENTS

3 tablespoons olive oil
12 ounces skinned chicken breast
fillets, cut into thin strips
1 bunch scallions, sliced
1 fresh red chili, seeded and
chopped
1 red bell pepper, cut into thin strips
3 ounces fresh shiitake
mushrooms, sliced
3–4 tablespoons chopped fresh
cilantro
1 round of pizza dough, 10–12
inches in diameter
1 tablespoon chili oil
5 ounces mozzarella cheese
salt and freshly ground black
pepper

SERVES 3–4

2 Pour off any excess oil, then set aside to let the chicken mixture cool.

3 Stir the fresh cilantro into the cooled chicken mixture in the wok.

4 Brush all over the top of the pizza-dough round with the chili oil.

5 Spoon on the chicken mixture and drizzle with the remaining olive oil.

1 Heat 2 tablespoons olive oil in a wok or large frying pan. Add the chicken, scallions, chili, red pepper and mushrooms and stir-fry over high heat for 2–3 minutes, until the chicken is firm but still slightly pink inside. Season to taste.

6 Grate the mozzarella and sprinkle it over the pizza. Cook the pizza on a medium-hot grill for about 15–20 minutes, until the crust is crisp and golden and the cheese is bubbling. Serve the pizza immediately.

MEDITERRANEAN QUICHE

· · ·

This quiche forms the ideal basis for a hearty picnic feast. The strong Mediterranean flavors of tomatoes, peppers and anchovies complement the cheese pastry beautifully.

INGREDIENTS

FOR THE PASTRY
2 cups all-purpose flour
pinch of salt
pinch of dry mustard
8 tablespoons (1 stick) butter,
chilled and diced
2 ounces Gruyère, grated
salt and freshly ground black
pepper

FOR THE FILLING
2-ounce can anchovy fillets, drained
1/4 cup milk
2 tablespoons French mustard
3 tablespoons olive oil
2 large Spanish onions, peeled and
sliced
1 red bell pepper, very finely sliced
3 egg yolks
1 1/2 cups heavy cream
1 garlic clove, crushed
6 ounces sharp Cheddar cheese,
grated
2 large tomatoes, thickly sliced
2 tablespoons chopped fresh basil,
to garnish

SERVES 6–8

2 Add the Gruyère and process again briefly. Add enough ice water to make a stiff dough: the dough will be ready when it forms a ball. Wrap the dough in plastic wrap and chill in the refrigerator for at least 30 minutes.

3 Meanwhile, make the filling. Soak the anchovies in the milk for about 20 minutes to make them less salty. Pour off the milk. Heat the olive oil in a frying pan and cook the onions and red pepper until they soften.

1 To make the pastry, place the flour, salt and mustard in a food processor, add the butter and process the mixture until it resembles fine bread crumbs.

4 In a bowl, beat the egg yolks, cream, garlic and Cheddar cheese together; season with salt and pepper.

5 Preheat the oven to 400°F. Roll out the chilled pastry and use it to line a 9-inch quiche pan with a removable bottom. Spread the mustard over the pastry and chill for another 15 minutes.

6 Arrange the tomatoes in a layer in the pastry crust. Top with the onion and pepper mixture and the anchovy fillets. Pour on the egg mixture. Bake for 30 minutes. Serve warm or at room temperature, sprinkled with fresh basil.

Cook's Tip
Leave the quiche in its pan if you are packing it for a picnic.

CHICKEN AND APRICOT FILO PIE

。 。 。

The filling for this pie has a Middle Eastern flavor—ground chicken combined with apricots,
bulgur wheat, nuts and spices. It both looks and tastes spectacular.

INGREDIENTS

½ cup bulgur
6 tablespoons butter
1 onion, chopped
1 pound ground chicken
¼ cup dried apricots, finely
chopped
¼ cup blanched almonds, chopped
1 teaspoon ground cinnamon
½ teaspoon ground allspice
¼ cup strained plain yogurt
1 tablespoon snipped fresh chives,
plus extra to garnish
2 tablespoons chopped fresh
parsley
6 large sheets filo pastry
salt and freshly ground black
pepper

SERVES 6

1 Preheat the oven to 400°F. Put the bulgur in a large bowl with ½ cup boiling water. Allow the bulgur to soak for 5 minutes, until the water is absorbed.

2 Heat 2 tablespoons of the butter in a pan and fry the onion and chicken until pale golden. Stir in the apricots, almonds and bulgur and cook for another 2 minutes. Remove from the heat and stir in the cinnamon, allspice, yogurt, chives and parsley. Season to taste with salt and pepper.

3 Melt the remaining butter. Unroll the filo pastry and cut into 10-inch rounds. Keep the pastry rounds covered with a clean, damp dish towel to prevent them from drying out.

4 Line a 9-inch removable-bottomed tart pan with 3 pastry rounds, brushing each with butter as you layer them. Spoon in the chicken mixture and cover with 3 more pastry rounds, brushed with melted butter as before.

5 Crumple the remaining rounds and place on top of the pie. Brush with any remaining butter. Bake the pie for about 30 minutes, until the pastry is golden brown and crisp. Serve hot or cooled, garnished with fresh chives.

CHICKEN WITH FRESH HERBS AND GARLIC

A whole chicken can be roasted on a spit on the grill. This marinade keeps the flesh moist and delicious, and the fresh herbs add summery flavors.

INGREDIENTS

4½-pound free-range chicken
finely grated rind and juice of
1 lemon
1 garlic clove, crushed
2 tablespoons olive oil
2 fresh thyme sprigs
2 fresh sage sprigs
6 tablespoons unsalted butter,
softened
salt and freshly ground black
pepper

SERVES 4

1 Season the chicken well. Mix the lemon rind and juice, crushed garlic and olive oil together and pour them over the chicken. Let marinate in the refrigerator for at least 2 hours.

Cook's Tip

If roasting the chicken in the oven, preheat the oven to 450°F and reduce the heat to 375°F after 10 minutes. If you are roasting a chicken to serve cold, cooking it in foil helps to keep it succulent—open the foil for the last 20 minutes to brown the skin, then close it as the chicken cools.

2 Place the herbs in the cavity of the bird and smear the butter over the skin. Season well. Cook the chicken on a spit on the grill for 1½–1¾ hours, basting with the marinade, until the juices run clear when a thigh is pierced with a skewer. Let the bird rest for 15 minutes before carving.

PEPPER STEAK

• • •

This easy, rather indulgent bistro classic can be put together in a matter of minutes for an intimate summer supper in the garden. The creamy sauce helps to balance the heat of the pepper.

INGREDIENTS

2 tablespoons black peppercorns
2 tenderloin or boneless sirloin
steaks, about 8 ounces each
1 tablespoon butter
2 teaspoons olive oil
3 tablespoons brandy
2/3 cup whipping cream
1 garlic clove, finely chopped
salt, if necessary

SERVES 2

1 Place the black peppercorns in a sturdy plastic bag. Crush the peppercorns with a rolling pin or meat pounder until they are crushed to medium-coarse pepper.

2 Put the steaks on a chopping board and trim away any excess fat, using a sharp kitchen knife. Press the pepper firmly onto both sides of the meat, to coat it completely.

3 Melt the butter with the olive oil in a heavy frying pan over medium-high heat. Add the meat and cook for 6–7 minutes, turning once, until cooked to your liking. Transfer the steaks to a warmed platter or plates and cover to keep warm.

4 Pour in the brandy to deglaze the pan. Allow the brandy to boil until it has reduced by half, scraping the bottom of the pan, then add the whipping cream and garlic. Bubble gently over medium-low heat for about 4 minutes, or until the cream has reduced by about one-third. Stir any accumulated juices from the meat into the sauce, taste and add salt as necessary. Serve the steaks hot, with the sauce.

PORK WITH MARSALA AND JUNIPER

Sicilian marsala wine gives savory dishes a rich, fruity and alcoholic tang. The pork is fully complemented by the flavor of the sauce in this quick and luxurious dish.

INGREDIENTS

1 ounce dried cèpe or porcini
mushrooms
4 pork scallops
2 teaspoons balsamic vinegar
8 garlic cloves
1 tablespoon butter
3 tablespoons marsala
several rosemary sprigs
10 juniper berries, crushed
salt and freshly ground black
pepper

SERVES 4

1 Put the dried mushrooms in a large bowl and just cover with hot water. Let stand for 20 minutes to allow the mushrooms to soak.

2 Brush the pork with 1 teaspoon of the vinegar and season with salt and pepper. Put the garlic cloves in a small pan of boiling water and cook for 10 minutes, until soft. Drain and set aside.

3 Melt the butter in a large frying pan. Add the pork and fry quickly until browned on the underside. Turn the meat over and cook for 1 minute more.

4 Add the marsala, rosemary sprigs, drained mushrooms, 4 tablespoons of the mushroom water, the garlic cloves, juniper berries and the remaining balsamic vinegar.

5 Simmer gently for 3–5 minutes, until the pork is cooked through. Season lightly and serve hot.

STUFFED ROAST LOIN OF PORK

. . .

This recipe uses fruit and nuts as a stuffing for roast pork in the Catalan style. It is full of flavor
and is very good served cold, making an excellent centerpiece for a summer buffet or a picnic.

INGREDIENTS

4 tablespoons olive oil
1 onion, finely chopped
2 garlic cloves, chopped
1 cup fresh bread crumbs
4 dried figs, chopped
8 pitted green olives, chopped
¼ cup sliced almonds
1 tablespoon lemon juice
1 tablespoon chopped fresh parsley
1 egg yolk
2-pound boned loin of pork
salt and freshly ground black
pepper

SERVES 4

1 Preheat the oven to 400°F, or
prepare the grill. Heat 3 tablespoons of
the oil in a pan, add the onion and
garlic, and cook gently until softened.
Remove the pan from the heat and stir
in the bread crumbs, figs, olives,
almonds, lemon juice, chopped fresh
parsley and egg yolk. Season to taste
with salt and ground black pepper.

2 Remove any string from the pork
and unroll the belly flap, cutting away
any excess fat or meat to enable you to
do so. Spread the stuffing over the flat
piece and roll it up, starting from the
thick side. Tie at intervals with string.

3 Pour the remaining olive oil into
a roasting pan and put in the pork, or
arrange on the spit of the grill. Roast
for 1 hour and 15 minutes, or until the
juices from the meat run clear.

4 Remove the pork from the oven or
the spit and, if serving hot, let it rest for
10 minutes before carving into thick
slices. If serving cold, wrap the meat in
foil to keep it moist until you carve it.

LAMB CASSEROLE WITH GARLIC AND BEANS

This Spanish-influenced recipe makes a substantial meal when served with potatoes.
Fava beans add color and texture to the dish.

INGREDIENTS

3 tablespoons olive oil
3–3½ pounds lamb fillet, cut
into 2-inch cubes
1 large onion, chopped
6 large garlic cloves, unpeeled
1 bay leaf
1 teaspoon paprika
½ cup dry sherry
4 ounces shelled fresh or frozen
fava beans
2 tablespoons chopped fresh parsley
salt and freshly ground black
pepper

SERVES 6

3 Add the garlic, bay leaf, paprika and sherry. Season to taste and bring to a boil. Cover and simmer gently for 1½ hours, until tender.

4 Add the fava beans to the casserole and cook for another 10 minutes. Stir in the chopped fresh parsley just before serving.

1 Heat 2 tablespoons olive oil in a large flameproof casserole. Add half the meat and brown well on all sides. Transfer to a plate. Brown the rest of the meat in the same way and remove from the casserole.

2 Heat the remaining oil in the pan, add the onion and cook for about 5 minutes, until soft. Return the meat to the casserole.

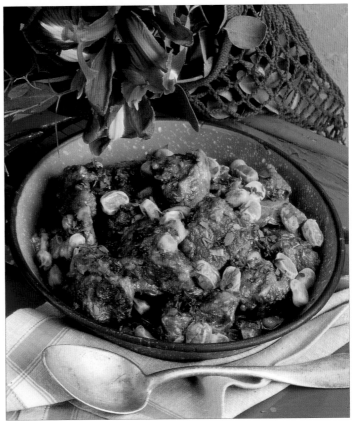

RED MULLET WITH LAVENDER

· · ·

Cook a fish dish with a difference by adding lavender to red mullet for a wonderful, aromatic flavor. Sprinkle some lavender flowers on the coals too, to give a delightful perfumed ambience.

INGREDIENTS

4 red mullet, scaled, gutted and cleaned
2 tablespoons olive oil

FOR THE MARINADE
3 tablespoons fresh lavender flowers or 1 tablespoon dried lavender leaves, roughly chopped
roughly chopped rind of 1 lemon
4 scallions, roughly chopped
salt and freshly ground black pepper

SERVES 4

1 Place the fish in a shallow dish. Mix the ingredients for the marinade and pour over the fish. Cover the fish with plastic wrap and let marinate in the refrigerator for at least 3 hours.

2 Remove the fish from the marinade and brush it with olive oil. Cook the fish on a hot grill for 10–15 minutes, turning once and basting with olive oil as they cook.

SALMON STEAKS WITH OREGANO SALSA

• • •

This combination of salmon with piquant tomato works incredibly well. The barbecue gives the salmon an exquisite flavor. Served hot or cold, this is an ideal dish for a summer lunch.

INGREDIENTS

1 tablespoon melted butter
4 salmon steaks, about 8 ounces each
1/2 cup white wine
freshly ground black pepper

FOR THE SALSA
2 teaspoons chopped fresh oregano, plus sprigs to garnish
4 scallions, trimmed
8 ounces ripe tomatoes, peeled
2 tablespoons extra virgin olive oil
1/2 teaspoon sugar
1 tablespoon tomato paste

SERVES 4

1 Butter 4 squares of double-thickness aluminum foil. Put a salmon steak on each and add a little wine and a grinding of black pepper. Wrap the salmon steaks loosely in the foil, sealing the edges securely. Cook on a medium-hot grill for 10 minutes, until just tender. If serving the steaks hot, keep them warm.

2 Put the chopped fresh oregano in a food processor and chop it very finely. Add the scallions, tomatoes and remaining salsa ingredients. Pulse until chopped but not a smooth purée.

3 Serve the salmon hot or cold with the salsa, garnished with a sprig of fresh oregano.

HERBAL PUNCH

This refreshing party drink will have people coming back for more, and it is an original non-alcoholic choice for drivers and children.

INGREDIENTS

2 cups honey
7 pints water
2 cups freshly squeezed lemon juice
3 tablespoons fresh rosemary leaves, plus extra to decorate
8 cups sliced strawberries
2 cups freshly squeezed lime juice
7½ cups sparkling mineral water
ice cubes
3–4 scented geranium leaves, to decorate

SERVES 30 PLUS

1 Combine the honey, 4 cups water, one-eighth (¼ cup) of the lemon juice and the fresh rosemary leaves in a saucepan. Bring to a boil and heat, stirring constantly, until the honey is dissolved. Remove from the heat and allow to stand for about 5 minutes. Strain into a large punch bowl and set aside to cool.

2 Press the strawberries through a fine sieve into the punch bowl, add the rest of the water and lemon juice, the lime juice and the sparkling mineral water. Stir gently to combine the ingredients. Add the ice cubes just 5 minutes before serving, and float the geranium and rosemary leaves on the surface.

MINT CUP

· · ·

Mint is a perennially popular flavoring, and this delicate cup is a wonderful mixture with an intriguing taste. It is the perfect summer drink to serve with meals outdoors.

INGREDIENTS

handful of fresh mint leaves
1 tablespoon sugar
crushed ice
1 tablespoon lemon juice
3/4 cup grapefruit juice
2 1/2 cups chilled
tonic water
mint sprigs and lemon slices,
to decorate

SERVES 4–6

1 Crush the mint leaves with the sugar and put into a pitcher. Fill the pitcher to the top with crushed ice.

2 Add the lemon juice, grapefruit juice and tonic water. Stir gently to combine the ingredients and decorate with mint sprigs and slices of lemon.

STRAWBERRY AND MINT CHAMPAGNE

· · ·

This is a simple concoction that makes a bottle of champagne or sparkling white wine go much further. It tastes very special on a hot summer evening.

INGREDIENTS

1¼ pounds strawberries
6–8 fresh mint leaves
1 bottle champagne or sparkling white wine
fresh mint sprigs, to decorate

SERVES 4–6

2 Strain through a fine sieve into a large bowl. Half-fill a glass with the mixture and top up with champagne or sparkling wine. Decorate with a sprig of fresh mint.

1 Purée the strawberries and fresh mint leaves in a food processor.

MELON, GINGER AND BORAGE CUP

· · ·

Melon and ginger complement each other magnificently. If you prefer, you can reduce or leave out the powdered ginger—the result is milder but equally delicious.

INGREDIENTS

½ large honeydew melon
4 cups ginger ale
1 teaspoon powdered ginger
borage sprigs with flowers, to decorate

SERVES 6–8

1 Discard the seeds from the half melon and scoop the flesh into a food processor. Blend the melon to a purée.

2 Pour the purée into a large jug and top up with ginger ale. Add powdered ginger to taste. Pour into glasses and decorate with borage.

NOTES

NOTES

NOTES

NOTES

NOTES

NOTES